A Good Goodbye

Funeral Planning for Those Who Don't Plan to Die

D0882270

Gail Rubin

ISBN-13: 978-0-9845962-0-1

Published by Light Tree Press
P.O. Box 36987
Albuquerque, NM 87176-6987
Telephone: 505-265-7215
www.LightTreePress.com

Praise for

A Good Goodbye

Funeral Planning for Those Who Don't Plan to Die

"*A Good Goodbye* thoroughly and impressively covers so much that families need to know about funeral planning. It's such a valuable resource, we have several copies in our library as a reference book for those we serve."

—Chester French Stewart, Chairman,
French Funerals-Cremations and
the French Family of Companies
Albuquerque, New Mexico

■

"With grace, humor, honesty, and skill, Gail Rubin shines a light on a subject that we, as a society, prefer to keep in the dark. Sooner or later, we will all need the information in *A Good Goodbye*, a highly readable, entertaining, and informative book."

—Jillian Brasch, author,
The Last Gifts

■

"Gail Rubin takes on society's last taboo in a readable, practical manner with a light touch. It's a great read for anyone who isn't sure about this 'death thing' and how to best prepare for it."

—Joe Sehee, Executive Director,
Green Burial Council

More Praise for
A Good Goodbye
Funeral Planning for Those Who Don't Plan to Die

"Kudos to Gail Rubin for pointing out the blue elephant in the corner. The earlier we can engage each other in end-of-life conversations, the better our chances for ending our lives the same way we lived them — with grace and intent. This book is filled to the brim with material to inspire those conversations."

—Alexandra Drane, Cofounder
Engage With Grace
and President of Eliza Corporation

■

"Gail Rubin is on a mission to demystify death care. This book represents the highest and best use of her experience and depth of knowledge on planning the ultimate in an end-of-life event, formerly known as a funeral."

—Brian J. Hanner CT, CPC, CFSP
Geib Funeral Homes, Crematories
& Remembrance Centers
Dover & New Philadelphia, Ohio

■

"*A Good Goodbye* has 'heart sense' in its how-to information that's vitally needed before there's a death in the family. Gail Rubin helps us face the thought of our death and better appreciate the reality of life."

—Thelma Domenici, Etiquette Advice Columnist,
The Albuquerque Journal

*This book is dedicated to all those who have
gone before to be our guides;
with special gratitude to Norman Bleicher,
Arthur Cohen, and Wesley Vincent.*

A Good
Goodbye

**Funeral Planning for Those
Who Don't Plan to Die**

Contents

Contents

3

We Can Do That?

New trends in death care

4

It's My Party and I'll Die If I Want To

Unique memorial ceremonies, remains disposal, and receptions

Contents

5

I Have Some Sad News

6

Lend Me Your Ears

7

Amazing Grace

Contents

8

I Got It at Costco
Minimizing funeral and burial costs 139

9

Where's Fido?
What to do when a pet dies..148

10

"What-If" Questions
Pondering out-of-the-ordinary situations 160

11

As Time Goes By

12

Just the Facts

Introduction

Over My Dead Body

Who's the funeral for, really?

"Dying is regarded as bad taste in this society, despite the fact that ten out of ten people do it."
— *Hemlock Society brochure*

In America, death is often regarded as the classic Monty Python routine about the Spanish Inquisition. "Nobody expects the Spanish Inquisition! Our chief weapons are fear, surprise, and an almost fanatical devotion to the Pope."

Death surprises and scares us. Despite the fact that humans have a 100 percent mortality rate, we don't expect to die. If you don't expect to die, you're unlikely to preplan a funeral. And that leads to problems like family discord, higher costs, rote rituals devoid of meaning, and unnecessary stress added to grief.

Everyone is too young to die. Cancer and other diseases claim both young and old before their time. Patients look to modern medicine to prolong life by any means. Teenagers, who think they're immortal, are devastated when a peer tragically dies in an auto accident, suicide, overdose, or some other mishap. Even the centenarians featured weekly on the *Today Show* will die some day.

We are mortal. Our bodies eventually stop working. Many religions teach that the soul, the spirit that resides within our bodies as long as we breathe, lives forever. So, why the fear of death, and by extension, of funeral planning?

To talk about funeral planning, we would have to admit that this joy ride called life has an end. We'd have to look at how we've lived our lives, examine how we've acted and review what we've done with our time on Earth. We'd be forced to look at how we've treated others, and think about what others would say about us at our funerals. We'd need to take stock of our achievements and contributions to humanity. Perhaps we are afraid we'll find ourselves lacking.

There are other reasons. Medical advances have saved so many lives so many times, it seems like death is optional. We don't like the thought of losing the company of those we love. We avoid thinking or talking about death, perhaps for fear that its contemplation will precipitate the event. And many folks just don't know what to do anymore when it comes to death.

Robert Fulghum, who wrote *All I Really Need to Know I Learned in Kindergarten*, also wrote a lovely book called *From Beginning to End: The Rituals of Our Lives*. He described visiting the Greek island of Crete, and witnessing a Greek Orthodox funeral there.

He wrote, "The religious customs of the Greek Orthodox Church so permeate the lives of people that when someone dies, everyone knows what is to be done and how to participate in it. Life and death are so carefully interwoven that the rites of passage from one to another are seamless and unquestioned."

We've lost that sense of what to do when there's a death in the community. Our pluralistic society is a good thing in many ways, but when it comes to death, funerals, and mourning, we've lost sight of many traditions we once had.

As Fulghum said, "For most of us, once we die, we are no longer in the care of our families and friends — strangers and institutions take over... Death is not in our school curriculum."

He added, "Instead of a normal part of life, death is treated as an unexpected emergency, something that happens when the medical community fails. We always die 'of something' — as though if it weren't for that disease or accident, we could have lived on. 'Old age' or 'worn out' or 'life completed' are concepts not found on death certificates or in obituaries. Death in our time means crisis."

Death is a very real part of life, along with taxes. Yet, funerals are the only life cycle event most folks don't want to plan in advance. Wedding planning gets way more attention than funeral planning, even though both events can conceivably cost the same, given a modest wedding and a traditional funeral. Yet, if the bride and groom planned their wedding the way most folks plan a funeral, they'd be scrambling to pull everything together in three days—talk about stress!

We use euphemisms for death: Passed on; kicked the bucket; gave up the ghost; checked out; left the building; keeled over; took the Big Bus; caught the last train; bought the farm; paid the ultimate price; pushing up daisies; knocking on the Pearly Gates; taking a dirt nap; and gone to the Great (whatever) in the Sky.

You, me, all humanity, we will all need to be disposed of when we die. If you don't talk about what you want done with your lifeless body, you will leave your family and friends in a world of hurt if the Big Bus unexpectedly runs you over tomorrow and transports you to the Pearly Gates. Do everybody a favor and make some plans. It's best to put your two cents in now, while you still can.

As journalist Eleanor Clift said in a *New York Times Magazine* interview, "It's time to take death out of the closet and talk about it and recognize the steps you need to take should some medical calamity befall you."

Why Have a Funeral or Memorial Service?

Maybe you don't care what people do about you after your death. After all, you won't be around to enjoy the party. But the people who love you care deeply.

My friend Gary, a confirmed bachelor in his sixties with no immediate family in the area, said that he doesn't want a funeral when he dies. To his way of thinking, he's not religious, doesn't like ceremonies or rituals, and doesn't want people to make a fuss. But so many of his friends will miss him and his warm wit, his deep intellect, his incredible guitar playing, and his appreciation of fine wine. Those who know him and call him a friend will want to honor his life, even though Gary pooh-poohs the idea.

My brother Mitch had a life partner named Wes who died from liver cancer in 2007. Within days, my brother and I, along with family and friends, planned a very moving memorial service that reflected the many unique aspects of Wes's life and character. "Wes explicitly said he didn't want a memorial service," said Mitch. "But we didn't do it for him; we did it for us."

Funerals, or memorial services if the body isn't present at the event, are not really for the person who has passed on and may or may not be observing the proceedings. These rituals provide the opportunity for family and friends to come together in support, remember and share stories about the dearly departed, and celebrate his or her character and contributions. Dispatching ceremonies provide an appropriate closing chapter in the book of that person's life.

"We need rituals, not just for the dead but for those of us who aren't yet dead, as well. I am weary of sweeping up the pieces for those family members who would not recognize a loss with a ritual," said Dr. William G. Hoy, a grief counselor and death educator.

He explained, "Very often — with those who don't stop and ritualize the death — six months later, these families are in my office, having a harder time with grieving and healing. My clinical experience matches fairly closely the experience I hear from colleagues. We need rituals to celebrate the life, to be sure, but also to socially acknowledge the death."

The bereavement process starts with the recognition and realization that someone has died. The funeral or memorial service provides an opportunity to *remember* and tell stories about the person, to come to terms with the *reality* of death, to *reaffirm* beliefs, and to *release* the spirit of the deceased. Remembering and reaffirming generate stories and laughter, realizing and releasing prompt healing tears and goodbyes.

Psychologists note a number of reasons why these rituals matter. They make the dead "safely dead," dispatched with proper ceremony to rest in peace. They confirm that the deceased and their survivors matter, and that the community will continue. They provide structure in the midst of chaos and disorder, and assure communal support for survivors during a stressful time.

Why Plan Ahead?

Here's a thought to consider. With a wedding, you have weeks, months, even years to plan, purchase, and implement all the aspects: clergy, location, communications to family and friends, flowers, clothing, music, food, transportation, and so on. With a funeral, you have only an average of twenty-four to seventy-two hours to make the same types of arrangements, while also dealing with the emotional impact of the loss of a loved one.

Planning a funeral right after a family member dies is probably the last thing you want to do. Hence, funeral directors are the equivalent of wedding planners for the last step in the life cycle, handling all those details for you. You still need to have basic facts about the deceased to process death certificates, and it would be comforting to know you are handling the disposal of the body the way that person would have wanted.

Jessica Mitford, author of the landmark book *The American Way of Death* published in 1963, told the story of President Franklin D. Roosevelt's unheeded last wishes. Roosevelt had written down instructions, but kept the document in his private safe. He wanted a simple, dark wood casket; no embalming; no hermetically sealed coffin; no grave lining; transportation by gun carriage, not by hearse; and no lying in state anywhere. The document was discovered a few days after his burial. Unfortunately, the only instruction followed was that he did not lie in state.

While conducting research for this book, my husband and I met with a mortuary to preplan funeral arrangements for my father-in-law, Norman. We were a bit surprised at how much information was needed, and glad to have the luxury of time and Norm's availability to provide more details. This was three years before he actually died. After he passed on, my mother-in-law, Myra, told us she disliked our proactive preplanning activities at the time. However, when the time came to put the plan into action, she was glad we had already done the work.

As columnist Ellen Goodman commented, "How many families actually have 'the talk,' something as dreaded as 'the talk' about sex? How many tiptoe around the questions that surround death, parents not wanting to upset children, children not wanting to upset parents? As if we were not in it together."

Goodman continued, "I have known experts who could speak in public on this subject but not to their mothers. No one is immune from denial — not even the anthropologist Margaret Mead, who preached the need for an open conversation about death. When her time came, and her daughter came to talk, Mead said she wasn't dying, she had too much left to do."

So how do you work this? At the most basic level, drop the denial. Recognize death is part of life. Start by letting your loved ones know how you want to be disposed of — burial, cremation, donating your body to science. Give them some sense of how you would like them to celebrate your life when you're gone. Let the family know if you prefer they hold a rowdy wake. But it requires more than just writing down your wishes — you need to talk to your people.

Mark Duffey, president and CEO of Everest Funeral Planning and Concierge Services, observed, "While no one likes to address the emotional aspects of death or a funeral head-on, most people are willing to discuss it openly and honestly when you frame it around facts and figures."

He added, "To kick-start the conversation, you can ask your loved one, 'If you were to be hit by a bus tomorrow, what would you want us to do?' It's a question anyone, anywhere, and at any age, can relate to. Keep in mind, though, it's always best to have the conversation when there are no health issues out there already. It's also important to understand that the answer is really for the person asking the question, not for the person being asked."

Sometimes, the best way to move recalcitrant parents or spouses along on preplanning is to make your own arrangements first. That's what my husband and I did, telling his parents we were going cemetery plot shopping and asking if they wanted to come along. They came, they saw, they bought, and it was easy. Or you might start the conversation by saying, "I know you plan to live forever, but accidents happen. Do you have any preferences for what you want done with your body?"

When you prepare for your own funeral, you can shape the show — sometimes with memorable, if unintended, consequences. I attended an elderly woman's graveside funeral, held on a very cold, snowy afternoon. One of her daughters gave the eulogy, and she shared her mother's last instructions. "Mom wanted to be buried wearing her socks and slippers, and covered by a favorite blanket, because she was always cold," she recalled. The mourners laughed knowingly when the daughter said that Mom had strong opinions and often got her way.

The daughter had done all as instructed. After the casket was lowered into the ground, the mourners sought the warmth of their cars. I lingered, gazing down into the stillness of the grave, leaning against the whipping wind, snow swirling around me. I thought, "Lady, you are warmer there six feet under than those of us above."

Why this Book?

The chapters that follow in *A Good Goodbye: Funeral Planning for Those Who Don't Plan to Die* will make it easier for you or your survivors to plan and implement a thoughtful, meaningful death ritual appropriate for each individual and family. With planning forms to help collect all needed information, we will sort out event planning under pressure, working with a funeral home, handling communications, minimizing costs, and putting together creative departures.

A survey by the Pew Forum on Religion and Public Life released in 2009 revealed that more than a quarter of adult Americans have left the faith of their childhood. Do you know your own religion's funeral traditions? If you married someone of another faith, do you know if your partner would want to follow such traditions and what would need to be done? What options do agnostics and atheists have? Funeral traditions practiced by Catholics, Protestants, Jews, Muslims, Buddhists, Hindus, plus other religions, are included to help you make informed choices in advance.

Young people have no interest in obituaries, unless a young celebrity meets an untimely end. As a boomer, I see contemporaries and the icons of our younger days showing up on the obituary page with increasing regularity. Like many folks on the upside of fifty, I now scan the obit page to see if anyone I know has died. This popular newspaper section also provides a rich source of information on funerals to attend for research. Good obituary writing is an art. We'll explore the differences between a news obituary and the information the bereaved put in the newspaper or that funeral directors place on their behalf.

A Good Goodbye also includes information on writing an ethical will, eulogies, and other memorial oratory. It's amazing what you can learn about a person at their funeral. The time to think about what you want said about you at yours is now. Your actions shape the legacy you will be remembered by.

A Good Goodbye incorporates creative and meaningful ways to remember and honor the deceased annually. It includes comments from clergy, funeral directors, and those on the cutting edge of new developments in addressing death. Pets are a part of the family, and we'll look at how to memorialize a beloved animal companion and ensure they are cared for if you go first.

Why Me?

As a columnist for the now-defunct *Albuquerque Tribune*, I wrote "Matchings, Hatchings, and Dispatchings," a how-to feature about local weddings, births, and deaths. The columns on death invariably elicited the greatest number of responses from readers who resonated with the information. To help people better handle the life cycle event associated with death, I have focused my efforts to show the many ways a final goodbye can be done well.

I am an event planner, not a psychologist. While researching this book, I have attended numerous funerals and memorial services, most for total strangers (not unlike the title characters in the cult classic film *Harold and Maude*). I am a member of the Association for Death Education and Counseling and the cemetery committee for my synagogue. I also volunteer for our local *Chevra Kaddisha*, a group that ritually prepares the bodies of Jews for burial.

I have had in-depth visits at mortuaries and the Office of the Medical Investigator, where I almost fainted from the smell. Television doesn't convey that aspect when you watch *CSI*. I have taken numerous courses on death rituals, grief, and the afterlife.

I'm also a breast cancer survivor. Nothing reminds you of your own mortality like a brush with something as serious and transforming as cancer.

The date and time of our eventual demise is a mystery. That uncertainty contributes to discomfort acknowledging our mortality. But facing the thought of our death can help us to better appreciate the reality of life.

Death can strike both the young and the old. Even when someone experiences a lingering illness, the end always seems unexpected. Attorney Randy Hamblin, speaking on estate planning at an end-of-life issues seminar, said, "Anyone younger than the age of seventy always prefaces their comments with 'If I die.' It's really 'When I die.' None of us are getting out of here alive."

I have seen and experienced the comfort that a funeral or memorial service can generate for those who grieve over a loved one who has died. My goal is to help you consider your role in this inevitable life cycle event, make it easier to implement the rituals that lead toward healing, and do it with humor.

We won't laugh in the face of death, but will approach the topic with a light touch to ward off despair and make the job of dispatching our loved ones easier to bear.

Come and take my hand. Don't fear the Reaper.

1

How Do I Work This?

Event planning under pressure

"Death is hacking away at my address book and party lists."
— Mason Cooley, US aphorist (1927–2002)

Someone you love has died. Who do you call first? What do you do next? How do you proceed through the next few days?

First, take a deep breath, and exhale. Don't forget to breathe! Your brain needs plenty of oxygen to cope with the emotions, the decisions to be made, and so many details to work out. Fundamentally, breathing is what sets the living apart from the dead. Don't hold your breath when faced with great challenges. Breathe.

From Death's Door

The countdown to a funeral or memorial service begins when a death is officially pronounced, stating the date, time, and cause of death. Nothing can be done with the body until pronouncement takes place, clearing the way for the preparation of a death certificate. After pronouncement, the body can be moved to begin preparing for final disposition.

In an unattended death, when a body is discovered and no one knows how the person died, the first call goes to police, who will involve the Coroners' Office or the Office of the Medical Investigator or Office of the Medical Examiner (OMI or OME). The coroner may take the body to their facilities, or with family involvement, a funeral home may take it.

If the coroner takes the body, they may perform an autopsy, or they may do a search of the person's medical records to determine a probable cause of death from preexisting conditions. The circumstances of the situation, state laws, the wishes of relatives, and religious/cultural dictates can also play a role in whether an autopsy is conducted.

In an "expected" death, one that happens, more often than not, in a hospital, nursing home, or hospice setting, a doctor or hospice nurse makes the pronouncement. Note that when a patient dies in a hospital, very often the family will be asked about organ donation, even if the patient was extremely old and you'd think no one would want their organs.

The staff may also ask about removing a pacemaker, which may be used to help ailing animals. This happened with my father-in-law, who was eighty-two when he died in the hospital, and that's exactly what my mother-in-law said: "Who would want them?" His organs, and his pacemaker, were left in his body.

The family needs to know in advance if the deceased wants their organs donated. Some states have laws that require hospitals to ask the organ donation question. This is when documents like advance medical directives come in handy. The organ donation question does not come up when a hospice patient dies, because quality can't be assured, and organ harvesting in a home death setting is problematical.

To facilitate pronouncement, the first call in an "expected" death goes to the primary doctor or hospice provider for the deceased; however, emergency room doctors can also record pronouncement. The second call would be to a funeral director, if previous arrangements have been made. If arrangements aren't already in place, a boatload of decisions will need to be made under duress.

Chances are, you'd be in the same boat with an "unexpected" death, such as an auto accident, suicide, homicide, when a person under the age of eighteen dies, or a body is discovered under mysterious circumstances. A police officer, coroner, or medical investigator will make the pronouncement to the best of their ability given the circumstances.

In most states, by health code, a body has to be processed within twenty-four hours — before decomposition begins — in one of four ways: refrigerate, embalm, cremate, or bury. Some states dictate a body may not be processed for disposition for forty-eight hours, usually in states that have coroners instead of medical examiners. This is to prevent disposition before an inquest can be raised if the death involved questionable circumstances. Embalming and refrigeration give the family a few more days with the body before cremation or burial, allowing distant relatives to travel for a funeral.

Both Jews and Muslims traditionally are prohibited from embalming and those religions dictate burial within twenty-four hours. However, individual and family customs can vary. Brian Hanner, a funeral director with Geib Funeral Homes in Ohio, said, "I never cease to be amazed by how widely traditions can vary, just based on geographical practice."

The funeral director prepares death certificates, with information completed by a medical certifier — a doctor, coroner, or other medical examiner. You might be surprised at the information you need to supply about the deceased. In addition to their legal name, you need any AKAs (also known as), Social Security number, birth date and place, marital status at death, mother's name prior to first marriage, military service discharge information, and more. A full listing of information usually requested for a death certificate is included among the forms in Chapter Twelve, "Just the Facts."

At-Home Death on Hospice Care

If a loved one dies at home on hospice care, the first call goes to the hospice organization. All hospice programs have registered nurses on call 24/7, and in most states, specially certified nurses may officially pronounce the deaths of home hospice patients. Check with a local provider to make sure this is the case in your state.

It helps to have a funeral home already selected to call after pronouncement, even if you haven't made funeral plans. The hospice nurse will call the funeral home of choice to take the body to their facility. Most mortuaries handle transportation of a body from the home in unmarked vans, not in a hearse.

While waiting for the mortuary, the nurse will offer to wash the body to the extent necessary or desired by the family, and remove catheters, IVs, or medicated patches. The family can help with the washing, if they wish.

Most state Board of Pharmacy rules prohibit hospice nurses from taking back leftover narcotics. The current procedure is for the nurse to tally up and destroy, with a family member as witness, any controlled substances the patient was taking, such as narcotics and sedatives. This is done by pouring the pills and liquids into a sealable plastic baggie, pouring cooking oil, vinegar, kitty litter, or bleach over them, and discarding the bag in the trash. "Flushing medications down the toilet is 'out' these days, to protect groundwater and river quality," said Nancy Costea, a hospice nurse.

If a patient has had a recent fall with an injury that might have contributed to the death, such as a hip fracture, the nurse will have to call OMI or the coroner's office. The investigator on duty will determine over the phone if they need to take the case. If so, OMI's removal team will take the body to their facility. OMI is also called if there's suspicion of abuse or neglect, or if circumstances point toward a drug overdose.

A word about DO NOT RESUSCITATE (DNR) orders: People who go on hospice acknowledge that they are going to die. Under current Medicare regulations, hospice providers cannot require that a DNR document be signed and in place. However, most hospice programs strongly encourage taking that step. This means that no heroic measures will be taken to restart heartbeat or breathing when the patient starts to fail.

Family members should *not* call 911 when the end seems near. Even with a DNR order, once emergency medical services are called, a home death gets needlessly complicated. Keep the hospice phone number posted by or programmed into the phone, and make sure anyone staying with the patient is aware of the importance of calling for the hospice nurse, *not* 911.

Next Steps to Take

Before forging ahead with arrangements, decide who's in charge of coordinating everything. Typically, the person put in charge of funeral arrangements is the closest living next of kin. This designation can vary by state, and can be superseded by power of attorney or estate representative designations. I suggest the person who is most level headed and the best event planner take the lead.

If an elderly parent has died and you're an only child, the surviving spouse, if there is one, may look to you to carry that load. If you have siblings, a family meeting to decide who will play what roles is in order. If your significant other or a child of yours has died, most likely you will be the one to make arrangements, but take advantage of assistance offered by those close to you.

If the deceased and the family are religious, you'll want to contact clergy quickly to get that support system started and coordinate with the church or synagogue on scheduling funeral events. Most clergy who know the deceased will drop what they're doing to address the family's needs, but as with a wedding, it's preferable to give the most time you can to prepare a funeral.

The next calls go to close family members and friends to give them the news and any information on developing plans for a funeral. Funeral planning doesn't necessarily mean you're holding a funeral. Each end-of-life event is different, with elements you can choose to do, or not. Your family traditions, religion, and individual beliefs will help guide your choices. Here's a quick outline of choices:

- **Funeral:** A service usually held within a week of death with the body present, followed by burial, entombment, or cremation. Viewing the body is optional. Sometimes called a memorial service.
- **Memorial Service:** A service held without the body present, or with cremated remains, within a flexible time schedule — often within a week of death, but sometimes weeks or months later.
- **Visitation:** One or more opportunities for community, relatives, and friends to visit the bereaved family; usually held at the funeral home prior to a funeral. Visitations often include viewing of the body, if that is the family's tradition. Catholics may incorporate a rosary service with eulogies as part of a visitation.
- **Burial/Entombment:** If the funeral is held anywhere other than graveside, a procession of funeral attendees

will follow the body to a cemetery. A separate ceremony is held to commit the body to its final resting place.

- **Reception:** After the ceremony, the family may host, or friends may help provide food, for a post-funeral or memorial service gathering. Also called a repast (African American or Pennsylvania Dutch tradition).

Within these end-of-life event elements, there is a wide range of options that influence costs, the meaningfulness of the ceremony, and how well the family starts to process their grief.

Event Planning Tools

Organization is a key component to putting a funeral or memorial service together without losing your mind. To do the best job possible with minimal stress, make sure you have the following tools in your event-planning arsenal.

Contact database – When there's a death in the family, how are you going to get in touch with all the people you need to call? You probably don't have all their numbers programmed into your phone's speed dial. And even if you did, how will you keep track of who's been contacted with the news? How will you delegate the task of calling people? This is a vital time to use a print-based system to manage your communications.

Before personal computers and cell phones became widely used, contact information for family and friends was most likely kept in Mom's dog-eared personal phone book in the kitchen drawer. You may still be using that paper system, and as long as information is kept up to date, use that resource!

If you are planning ahead before someone dies, or planning a guest list for a wedding or other big party, you can take personal phone book information and put it into a spreadsheet or database program. Contact information can be set up so the data can be manipulated into many different forms for various uses.

Names, addresses, phone numbers, emails, and other information can be used to keep track of who has been contacted, who sent cards or gifts, and if the giver was thanked and when. Phone lists and email blasts can be created with specific parameters when fast communication is a priority. Mailing labels can be pulled from the database for sending thank you notes.

This information needs to be updated regularly to stay useful. Update changes in address, phone, and email as soon as you hear about them. Remove the listings of those who have died and update the information for those who have moved, changed emails, or changed domestic partners. With regular maintenance, updating the data remains a small job.

Calendar – Calendars help you map out your timeline of actions to prepare for the funeral or memorial service. Take into consideration the day, as well as the date. Holidays, both secular and religious, can impact your plans. Variables between weekdays and weekends, such as overtime, changes in business hours, or religious mandates for a day of rest, may require changes to plans.

Timeline – Timelines provide a framework for actions to be implemented. For example, preparing the body for disposition and establishing a date, time, and place for services always come before making calls or placing obituaries. If a clergyperson will be involved, his or her schedule needs to be taken into consideration before setting a date and time.

To-do Checklist – This list contains action items that need to be accomplished, and who will do them. A checklist facilitates attention to details that might otherwise fall through the cracks. A sample checklist is included at the end of Chapter Two, "A Grave Undertaking."

Human Resources

Family and friends can be helpful allies in preparing life celebration events. They can handle event details, contribute musical or artistic talents, and provide moral support or referrals to reputable service providers. If someone asks how they can help, give them something specific to do, such as making calls to people about the service, or answering the phone for you while you handle other details. Ask those who have special talents to use their gifts in support of the event.

If you plan to have cousin Benny play classical guitar or ask artistic sister Susie to prepare a montage of family photos for your father's funeral, give them as much lead time as possible. Remember the niceties of saying "please" and "thank you" when you make your request. While not paid, family should be treated as professionals, since the services you are asking them to render are of professional caliber.

Working with Clergy

Life cycle events allow clergy to connect with their flock on a personal level. Matchings, hatchings, and dispatchings — weddings, births, and deaths — are a key part of their ministerial duties. Clergy can be enormously helpful with their insights and guidance for planning a funeral or memorial service. If there is a particular priest, pastor, or rabbi with whom you wish to work, contact that person or their assistant to check on availability before making any other arrangements.

If you are affiliated with a church or synagogue, the staff can offer general information, as well as observances specific to the congregation. The administrative staff helps make arrangements for on-site funerals and receptions in the congregation's social hall, which often have much of the equipment needed for entertaining. Check if the congregation charges fees for holding funeral events there.

For interfaith couples that have different religious backgrounds, funerals present a bump in the road. When there's a death, how will you decide what, if any, rituals will be followed? Think ahead and share your wishes with family members. A wide range of religious traditions associated with death is covered in Chapter Seven, "Amazing Grace."

The dilemma of observing different religions can also arise within the same family, if a branch of the family tree or a younger generation decides to "leave the church" for another house of worship. Expressing your wishes before the need arises may help avoid conflicts. You might talk about it around the dinner table at a family gathering, such as Thanksgiving or a major holiday.

If your family get-togethers are stressful affairs, you might think about writing and mailing letters after the holiday. You can state your preferences related to your funeral, final disposition, and religious or nonreligious observances to siblings, adult children, and living elders. An example of this kind of note:

Dear Joe:

It was so good to see you and the whole family at Thanksgiving. There's something I wanted to bring up, but it never seemed to be the right moment. I'd like everyone to know what my preferences are regarding a funeral, whenever my time comes.

Please work with Pastor Smith at our church. I'm fine with her doing a traditional church service. I haven't purchased any burial plots. I'd like to be cremated and have my ashes scattered in the lake where we spend every summer. It's so beautiful and peaceful there.

Please don't worry that I'm thinking about going anywhere soon. My health is fine. I just wanted you to know what my preferences are, so the family can be prepared whenever my number comes up. I look forward to spending many more years on planet Earth.

Love, Beth

Just a few lines with a touch of humor — indicating religion and disposition preferences — can make a big difference in family discourse when the time comes to move on. And you might get some interesting phone calls in response, opening the door to honest communications.

2

A Grave Undertaking

Working with a funeral home

"You always said you'd never be caught dead in a suit and tie.
Don't be."
Reflections Funerals and Life Celebrations brochure
Albuquerque, New Mexico

In ancient times, and even well into the twentieth century, a family was responsible for preparing the body and burying their own deceased. How times have changed! Most families today pay a funeral home to "undertake" those services, hence the origination of the term undertaker.

Over the last 150 years, the scope of funeral services has grown from humble origins to a multibillion-dollar industry. It evolved, starting with woodworkers who made coffins to supplement the furniture and cabinets that they made, and gravediggers hired to hand-dig burial sites. Today's death-care industry encompasses embalming, cosmetic work, cremation, cemeteries, memorial stones and plaques, transportation of bodies, caskets and urns made of metal, wood, and other materials, and a staggering array of other services.

Funeral directors can handle whatever arrangements you choose for burial or cremation — a memorial service, transporting the body, police escorts for funeral processions, flowers, receptions, and more. When you go into their offices, it helps to know in advance the many decisions that need to be made to arrange a funeral or memorial service for a loved one. Let's look at the details that need to be addressed.

Pre-Need Shopping Around: Part One

Shopping for a funeral when you don't need one is better than when you do need one. With the luxury of time, you can get the best deal possible. It's a fascinating shopping trip. My friend Gary, the one who doesn't want a fuss when he dies, went with me on shopping excursions to several local funeral homes. He wanted a cheap, simple, prepaid cremation, so everything would be taken care of when the time comes.

Yet, his plain request had a $750 price variation between providers for essentially the same services. The difference was due to overhead for the upscale funeral home setting of the highest priced provider.

We found funeral directors can have a great sense of humor, when there's no death imminent. When someone has recently died, or is about to die, the conversation has an appropriately somber tone. While meeting with one funeral director in an upscale funeral establishment, Gary and I were having a jolly conversation about cremated remains and the wide variety of disposal methods one can pursue with cremains, as they are called.

While we were talking and laughing, another funeral director came and quietly closed the door to the conference room we occupied. It turned out a bereaved family was sitting in the lobby right next to the room, and our lighthearted banter stood in stark contrast to their grief. I imagined the conversation those folks would have was not going to be remotely as pleasant as ours.

Another reason to shop around early: you realize the range of information needed for making final arrangements and can calmly collect that data without pressure. The details needed to complete a death certificate for a family member are not usually common knowledge. Quick, rattle off a spouse, parent, or sibling's Social Security number or place of birth! A form for collecting needed information is included in Chapter Twelve, "Just the Facts."

You will need to make decisions about the disposition of the body, if there will be services and when, if the body will be displayed, and what clothing or jewelry will be used. Choices also need to be made regarding flowers, music, readings, pallbearers, information for the obituary, and special instructions, such as donations in lieu of flowers. The list of "50 Things that Must Be Done When a Death Occurs" at the end of this chapter gives you a good idea of the many arrangements that await the family of the deceased.

If you go to a pre-need meeting with knowledge of choices to make and meaningful elements, you can get a good handle on the costs and compare them with other providers.

Glenn Taylor, past president of Selected Independent Funeral Homes, an association of family-owned funeral homes, grew up in the business. He recommends finding a provider with whom you feel comfortable having an engaged and open conversation, as well as shopping for price.

"Prearrangement is free. It doesn't cost a dime to create a road map for your family and put your wishes and dislikes on file," Taylor said. "If a funeral home is running a pre-need program and they're not willing to talk to you about just a prearrangement without funding, you're in the wrong place."

Taylor said prearranging also enables the family to make the funeral or memorial service more personalized and meaningful. "If your first dealing with a funeral home is when the death occurs, it's more difficult to provide a unique experience that clearly reflects the life, the attitude, the perspective of that person. It's not that the funeral director can't do it — we can. But often, the family is not in an emotional position to provide us with the information we need to make that happen," he explained.

It helps for families to visit funeral homes with an idea of what they do and do not want, but also open to suggestions and advice. Funeral director Brian Hanner, who also writes the blog, Ask the Director, said, "We've been able to help families think more clearly about things. Funeral directors are people who want to help you do what's right, and are experts at doing this. Since most people don't get a lot of experience with funerals, I think that's where we're probably of most value to families."

Increasingly, more families are asking for elements that personalize the experience, although some ask with hesitation. Glenn Taylor commented, "I'm often surprised by the things that families ask if they can do, which, to us, are just routine. I think they think there's a funeral police somewhere. It is not about what the neighbors think. It is about what has meaning for you."

"There's nothing we like any better than a family that comes to us and says, 'We want to do something different,' because we can do it," Taylor assured. Taylor is a fourth-generation funeral director, and his grandmother, whom he described as "the typical white-haired, genteel Southern lady" was also a funeral director who knew the value of meeting the needs of families. She may have been among the original providers of personalized funerals. Whenever she was asked about doing something a bit different, he said her response was often, "If it's not illegal and not too immoral, we can do it."

Brian Hanner added, "If I had a nickel for every time I heard 'I didn't know you could do that' I'd be rich."

Choices to Make

Decomposition is a smelly, messy, germ-ridden process. While it's a part of the natural order of birth, growth, death, and decay, it still gives many folks the creeps. Prompt disposal of the body is the key to funeral practices of many cultures.

Throughout history, all civilizations developed ways to dispose of human remains into one of the four elements: earth, burial; fire, cremation; water, burial at sea; and most infrequently, air. With sky burials in Tibet, where the ground is rocky and fuel for fire scarce, bodies are placed on a mountaintop for birds of prey to eat the flesh. Then the bones are crushed, the birds have at it again, and any remains are dispersed by the wind and rain. Notwithstanding the film *Psycho* where the character Norman Bates mummified his mother, keeping the bodies of our loved ones around once they have given up the ghost is not an option.

Chances are, if you're working with a funeral home, you'll be considering burial or cremation. With both options, there are additional choices to make.

Viewings

Do you want to put the body on display before final disposition, either at a private viewing or at the funeral? Would *you* want your body put on display for people to look at? While no state in the US requires embalming, most funeral homes will suggest it for viewings at visitations or the funeral. You can ask for the body to be refrigerated, instead of embalmed, and kept cool with dry ice. Generally, viewings are avoided when a person has died violently, but funeral directors have been known to work wonders with makeup.

If so desired, the mortician can do additional services of embalming, cosmetic work, dressing the body, and positioning it in the casket. The body can be viewed at a visitation at the funeral home or other location, or within a funeral service. Funeral directors have long extolled the benefits of the last look to form a "memory picture" for mourners to process their grief, as some people need to see the body to begin processing the reality of the death.

"There are usually three types of learning styles: auditory, learning by listening; the kinesthetic learners, people who need to actually, physically touch; then there are the visual ones who need to see," said Gloria Salazar, Family Service Director with Reflections Funerals & Life Celebrations. "Some people need to see that there is a body, dead as it is, in a casket, to fully realize the person is in fact dead, to get to the final stages of acceptance."

Embalming

Embalming was first utilized broadly in the United States during the Civil War, when surgeon-embalmers utilized early chemical compounds, including mercury and arsenic, to preserve soldiers' bodies long enough to ship them from battlefields back to their families in primarily Union states. In the majority of the 20th century, a formaldehyde-based preservative was used, and current embalming practices lean toward utilizing a less toxic mix of chemicals. With the development of modern refrigeration techniques to delay decomposition, there's a reduced need for embalming.

Funeral homes may present embalming as if it is something they must do, but the Federal Trade Commission's Funeral Rule of 1984 dictates disclosure that embalming is not required. The funeral home's own policies may dictate embalming a body for viewing, but the body can be preserved with refrigeration or dry ice.

Again, no state laws order that a body be embalmed. It is another service the funeral home can charge you for, and it may not be needed. If you think you'll want a viewing, you may need to pay for either multiple days of refrigeration or embalming.

Embalming involves flushing out blood from the veins by replacing it with a chemical solution that temporarily preserves and disinfects the body. In addition, the abdominal organs are punctured, bacteria and visceral fluid are vacuumed out, and the area is filled with more chemical fluids. This treatment slows, but does not stop, decomposition of the body, and it can plump up the skin's appearance.

The religious traditions of Jews and Muslims prohibit embalming, as the blood is considered a part of the body to be buried with the deceased. In addition, nothing should be done to retard, or in the case of cremation, accelerate, the returning of the body into the earth. There's more information about these traditions in Chapter Seven, "Amazing Grace."

My friend Kathleen told me about the unique viewing her family had for her father, where embalming provided a great benefit. He died in 1987 of gallbladder cancer that had spread to his liver, rendering his skin jaundiced and deeply creased at the time of his death. The family didn't want a general viewing at the funeral, just a private one for immediate family the night before.

Her dad was an avid deer hunter and fisherman who rarely wore a suit. The family just couldn't see burying him in something he wouldn't have been comfortable in. They provided his favorite plaid shirt, jeans, and fishing hat to dress him for the viewing.

"The funeral director worked magic with embalming and makeup that restored Dad to a healthy-looking appearance," said Kathleen. "When my siblings and I saw him the night of the viewing, almost simultaneously we exclaimed, 'It looks like Dad's taking a nap!' It gave us such peace to see him at rest in the kind of clothes he was most comfortable in.'"

The family decided to share this peaceful vision with others and held a viewing the next day at the church just prior to the funeral service.

"When our bodies are ravaged by cancer, I think that's when funeral directors who are talented and gifted embalmers can do their best work," commented Brian Hanner.

Cremation: Part One

About a third of the US population currently opts for cremation, and that percentage is projected to climb to 58 percent by 2025, according to the Cremation Association of North America. Cremation costs less than a traditional funeral, often thousands of dollars less, depending on other services selected. Cremains don't need to be buried in a cemetery, and scattering options abound.

Cremation involves reducing the body to grit by exposing it to high heat and flame in a special furnace called a retort, which generates temperatures of 1,600 to 1,800 degrees Fahrenheit. A family member must first visually identify the body before it is cremated, and authorize cremation, because it is irreversible. The funeral home must obtain the exact legal name of the deceased for the death certificate — no nicknames. The body is tagged with a metal disc that identifies the deceased and survives the fire. Pacemakers are removed before cremation, as they can explode in the retort.

A container must be used to put the body into the retort, usually either a cardboard box or a wooden casket built for cremation. Those who want a funeral with an open casket followed by cremation have the option of rental caskets, designed with removable beds and liners that are combustible.

Within two hours, flesh is reduced to an ash residue, leaving a brittle skeleton, which is then pulverized. Any dental work, joint replacements, or medically implanted pins and screws that survive the fire are screened out of the remains. The most basic container for cremains from the retort is a heavy plastic bag in a cardboard box that's about eight inches square.

In most states, the local county medical examiner's office, or sometimes the local Health Department, must issue a certificate before cremation can occur. This step is taken to ensure cremating the body will not prematurely destroy evidence that may be needed in a criminal case. The additional fee for cremation permits can range from $50 to $250.

Funeral homes offer a wide range of memorial containers to hold cremated remains: decorative urns of metal, stone, ceramic, wood or other materials, as well as biodegradable containers that can be used for burial or a send-off in a body of water.

Cremains can be buried or placed in a niche or columbarium in a memorial park, scattered on land or in water, kept in a box or urn at home, distributed among family members, or treated in a number of creative ways that reflect the personality of the deceased. Check out creative disposal methods in Chapter Four, "It's My Party and I'll Die If I Want To."

Donating the Body: Part One

Donating your body to science has a nice ring to it, but you need to decide that's what you're going to do before you die, because preregistration is a must with most medical school programs. It would also be wise to carefully study just how the body will be used in the name of science. One Ohio State University study used cadavers in place of crash test dummies to study the effect of dropping bodies from different elevations. Most donors do not have this type of use in mind when they sign up for medical donation.

There is no cost to donate one's body for medical research, but if a funeral home is involved, there may be some transportation fees. Make sure you have a "Plan B" if the medical school won't take the body due to trauma, obesity, or other reasons. You can read more about medical body donation in Chapter Eight, "I Got It at Costco," on minimizing funeral and burial costs.

A Word About Life Insurance

If you're like many people, you think a life insurance policy will pay for your funeral. Well, yes, it can — eventually. You may not realize it, but the money from a life insurance policy usually doesn't become available until an official death certificate for the insured person is issued by the state. That can take weeks or even months to process.

Families who count on life insurance to cover funeral expenses may have to scramble to cover costs right after someone dies, either through personal savings, credit cards, or borrowing from family and friends. Think about it — could your credit limit handle a charge of $8,000 to $10,000 for the products and services of a funeral home and cemetery? They won't bury your loved one without payment upfront.

But things are changing in regard to life insurance and funerals. Some life insurance companies now offer expedited payment of death benefits, reduced from months or weeks to days, a major shift to help their customers during one of the most stressful times in their lives.

In 2010, Aetna and The Hartford insurance companies introduced expedited payment of death benefits to beneficiaries of their group life insurance policies offered through employers. Both offer concierge funeral planning services through Everest, an independent consumer advocate for funeral-related issues. Everest helps the insured and their beneficiaries make advance funeral plans: reducing costs, providing family assistance, getting information on file for survivors, and recording ideas and preferences to help create a meaningful, memorable send-off ceremony.

The service is available to workers at no additional cost through employers, who use these companies' life insurance coverage as part of their employee benefit packages.

Scott Beeman, head of Aetna Life Insurance, said, "At a time of need, by expediting the claim payment, and having a funeral concierge there, we remove two barriers that prevent most people from being able to emotionally heal themselves and their families — their focus on the financials and the planning activities."

The Pros and Cons of Pre-Need Payment

Preplanning a funeral does not necessarily mean it's prepaid. There are arguments to be made both for and against prepayment. Bear in mind that the cost of a traditional funeral in 2010 ranges from $6,000 to $12,000, plus additional expenses for a cemetery plot and grave opening and closing, obituaries, receptions, etc. According to one funeral home representative I interviewed, funeral costs increase an average of six percent each year.

On the plus side, prepaying guarantees that the wishes of the deceased are honored, as they themselves select what they want and pay for it. It saves the family or legal representative the cost and anxiety of last-minute decision making in the midst of grief. Providers claim prepayment offers built-in inflation protection, assuring that the cost of the funeral will not increase, whether death occurs in three months or thirty years. If a family needs to reduce financial assets to qualify for Medicaid, one accepted way is to prepay for a funeral and burial plot.

There are several ways to save up the money to pay for a funeral, besides purchasing life insurance. You can set money aside in a joint account that can be accessed by the survivor to pay for a funeral. You can set up a Totten trust account, which is a separate insured and dedicated bank account specifically for funeral and burial costs that keeps these assets out of probate and available for use with a minimum of formalities.

A funeral insurance policy, also called burial or pre-need insurance, designed specifically to cover final arrangements, is another route. It names the selected funeral provider as the recipient of the funds, as opposed to a life insurance policy that provides funds to the family to use for final expenses and more.

If a loved one dies with no financial support in place for a funeral, there's the option of putting expenses on a credit card and use the airline miles to take a much-needed vacation. That's what Jackie Speier did, detailed in her book *This Is Not the Life I Ordered*. After her husband unexpectedly died, she put funeral expenses, including the headstone, on a credit card that gives airline rewards. She got enough mileage credit to take her two children to Hawaii, enabling her to de-stress from the shock. This assumes you've got a high enough credit limit to cover the costs.

Whatever financial road is taken, the family must be made aware of what arrangements and payments have been made — don't assume the funeral home staff will know.

Some things to consider before purchasing a prepaid funeral, courtesy of Connecticut's Attorney General:

- **Get the prices of the goods and services.** A copy of the general price list must be provided. You can get it in person or ask for the prices on the phone.
- **Get the separate price lists for caskets, vaults, and cremation urns.** These lists must also be provided.
- **Get a written statement of the goods and services you select.** This is important for comparison shopping and holding the funeral home accountable. (This also avoids any misunderstandings between your family and the funeral home when Mom says, "Everything's taken care of.")
- If you choose to take care of some services yourself, check to see if there are charges for these services in the fees. **Ask the funeral director to explain the services** included in the funeral home's fees and **insist the fee be reduced** if you make any of the arrangements yourself.
- It is not always clear what goods or services are guaranteed, or how excess funds will be handled. **Be sure that any contract you sign clearly specifies the responsibilities of the funeral home.**
- **Ask the funeral director to describe the investment risk and rate of return of every option.** Funds placed in escrow for prepaid funeral contracts should be managed as carefully as any other investment you make.
- **Contact the escrow agents directly** to ask about their management policies. Most must contact the consumer within 30 days of deposit.

And after purchasing:

- Give a trusted relative, friend, lawyer, or doctor a copy of the contract.

- If you go to a nursing home or hospital, give them a copy of the contract and name of the funeral home.

On the minus side, people have been harmed by prepaying for a funeral to a specific provider and to some funeral insurance companies. If the person moves to another state, the services that have been paid for may not be transferable. The money may be lost if a corporation buys up the funeral home and then doesn't honor the contract.

Funeral director Brian Hanner recommends checking the A.M. Best rating of funeral insurance companies and only doing business with an "A" rated company or better. Companies that are not rated by A.M. Best, or have a lower than "A" rating, are among those firms that give the industry a black eye.

Buying a funeral insurance contract is supposed to prevent the problems of prepaying to one provider. But, buyer beware. Some funeral insurance outfits have taken people's money and not provided paid-for services. In 2008, National Prearranged Services, Inc., a St. Louis-based seller of prepaid funeral plans, went into receivership when its financial reserves fell short of covering the costs of the funeral packages it had sold. Hundreds of funeral homes in at least nineteen states were affected by the financial meltdown.

Funeral director Glenn Taylor commented, "The only reason they won't make good is if they simply cannot afford to stay open, and that's not something we see very often. I would be most disappointed and frankly surprised if most funeral homes didn't honor their responsibility."

The Funeral Consumers Alliance, a nonprofit organization dedicated to protecting a consumer's right to choose a meaningful, dignified, and affordable funeral, recommends preplanning, but not prepaying. Their motto: "It always pays to plan ahead. It rarely pays to pay ahead."

Allan Levine has seen many emotional, panicked, last minute funeral arrangements during his fifty plus years' experience running temple cemeteries in Massachusetts and New Mexico. His advice on preparing for the inevitable, if you're going to be buried, is to buy a plot before you need it, but not necessarily paying for a funeral on a pre-need basis. He recommends writing down instructions that can be given in advance to clergy and the funeral director with all the information needed to prepare and implement a funeral.

"I'm definitely in favor of pre-need understanding, and it makes a lot of sense if there are children involved," Levine said. "I know of cases where families have stopped talking to each other because of disagreement over how to face death or a funeral."

Glenn Taylor agreed. "It's really important people understand that prearrangement is just that. It can be prefunded, as well, but it does not have to be," he claimed.

Caskets

"Just a simple casket, that's all I want," my father-in-law told me. That's not a whole lot of direction when you want to preplan a funeral for someone. Although he was still alive at the time to provide more input, he wasn't very forthcoming. I'm reminded of the plague victim in *Monty Python and the Holy Grail*, who said, "I'm not dead yet."

Per my father-in-law's directions, my husband and I looked at the simplest casket offered, but we actually chose a better-than-basic model. The simplest one had no handles, and we knew our pallbearers would need something to grab onto besides the bottom of the box.

The importance of handles was reinforced by a graveside funeral I witnessed, where middle-aged pallbearers struggled to carry a casket with no handles from the hearse to the grave. They had no way to get a good grasp, and when the burden got too heavy, they set it down above the grave in a spot where it got caught on the webbing that would lower the casket. The assembled mourners collectively held their breath watching the coffin precariously tip on the supports over the grave as the pallbearers tried to slide the box without pinching their fingers on the rollers below.

You can keep it simple, but whatever you do, get handles!

Funeral providers offer a wide range of caskets for burial, ranging from high-end metal with fine fabric linings, to elegant hardwoods or simple pine, to a growing number of "green" caskets designed to break down into organic matter along with the body. Caskets can be personalized with the colors and logo of a favorite sports team or other interests of the deceased. Cultural background, religious dictates, past funeral experiences, and your budget influence the type of casket, indeed the whole range of funeral services, you choose.

You do have options for where you buy a casket. A Federal Trade Commission ruling made it illegal for any funeral home to refuse a casket purchased from an outside source, charge a handling fee for it, or pressure a buyer against using a coffin purchased elsewhere. Brian Hanner commented, "I don't feel this way, but some funeral directors compare the idea of you bringing your own casket to a funeral home to someone bringing their own meal to a restaurant."

Outside casket providers include discount online sources and individual wood workers. Many providers ship on short notice, but waiting for the delivery of a coffin when you need it immediately is a nerve-wracking ordeal.

Remember, it's important to shop around before you need a casket. French Mortuary estimates that the average spent on a casket in 2010 is $2,497. A mind-boggling array is available, and trying to pick one out under the duress of grief is akin to buying a car in one afternoon without research because the auto you've been driving for years suddenly died. You may get buyer's remorse as soon as you drive off the lot and wonder if you paid too much.

Choosing a Final Resting Place

Even with the current rates of cremation, right now more than 50 percent of those who die in the US are going to be buried. Do you have plans for your body's final resting place? If burial is the way you want to go, this is something you don't want to leave up in the air.

Those with a religious affiliation can opt to be buried in "consecrated ground," a cemetery operated by their church or synagogue. There are many commercial cemeteries with no religious affiliation where anyone can purchase a plot. Military veterans, their spouses, and minor-age children can obtain free burial plots in national cemeteries (more on veterans' benefits later in this chapter).

And there are green burial grounds becoming established around the country. Some of these resting places are left in a natural state, where memorial markers are native stone chiseled with inscriptions, and burial services celebrate life and death within the cycles of nature.

Cemeteries usually operate separate from funeral homes, although some companies own both and can equally handle funeral and burial arrangements. More often, costs for grave opening and closing, grave liners, memorial markers, and vaults are separate and in addition to goods and services provided by the funeral home.

With a casket, vault, and grave liner, some burials can resemble those Russian stacking dolls, with a body in a box, within a box, within a box. A burial vault—which can be made of concrete, plastic, or metal—serves as a complete outer enclosure for the casket. A burial liner, made of concrete or plastic, protects only the top and sides of a casket. Liners, as well as vaults, keep the ground level and prevent the grave from sinking over the course of time.

Many cemeteries began requiring burial vaults after World War II, because around that time older monuments started heaving as graves collapsed and cemeteries started getting bad publicity about upkeep.

The use of grave liners is typical only in America where heavy equipment is used in cemeteries. In Europe, they simply pile more earth upon the grave or fill depressions as the ground settles.

You don't have to be put in the ground. Mausoleums, buildings with crypts that entomb the casket, keep the remains aboveground. Cremated remains can be parked in a columbarium, an aboveground monument with niches for the entombment of cremains, or placed in gardens created specifically for scattering ashes.

One caution about buying a plot in today's mobile society: If you move, you can't take it with you. You'll either need to sell the plot or have your body shipped back for burial when the time comes. Think your kids, who are now living in towns across the country, will want to be buried in a family plot? Better talk it over before investing in cemetery spaces on the assumption that your children will want to return to the fold. You may be in for a rude awakening.

Selling commercial cemetery plots can be difficult, as most for-profit cemeteries won't buy the site back. However, church- or synagogue-owned cemeteries may be a bit more lenient. My husband's parents had bought an extra plot from our congregation for his brother, Steven. There was no problem returning the unused plot and getting most of their money back when Steven got married and decided he would be buried elsewhere with his wife. Our congregation charges a 10 percent transaction fee on returned plots.

Another cemetery consideration is what's allowed regarding memorial markers. While some cemeteries continue to allow upright blocks of stone engraved with information, many now require memorial plaques that lie flat on the ground. By eliminating raised memorial stones, cemeteries can reduce the amount of time and money spent cutting the grass by driving one large mower across the graves and their markers. If you want an upright obelisk to mark your final resting place, make sure it's not against cemetery rules before you buy a plot.

What Do You Want on Your Tombstone?

There are plenty of decisions to make regarding a headstone, a product that's often, but not always, provided by a company other than the funeral home. Many cemeteries and funeral homes work with specific memorial marker manufacturers.

If you get a free marker for a veteran from the federal government, you must accept the established structure for name, rank, service branch, and date of birth and death. If you're ordering and paying for a memorial marker, there's a world of choices.

Some questions to be answered: Must the headstone be flat to the ground, and must it be of a specific size? This depends on the cemetery's rules and regulations. If a vertical marker is allowed, how big can it be and how much space can be used for words and images? Could one engrave on more than one side? Does the cemetery have a say over what words or images can be put on the memorial marker?

And oh, the choices! Do you want the marker to be metal or stone? If stone, such as granite, what color? Do you want to laser etch, sandblast, or hand-carve the stone? What kind of lettering style do you want to use? Do you want images, as well as words, engraved?

And what would you write for a term of endearment on an epitaph? Words have nuances on a headstone. "Beloved" implies the person was very much loved; "Devoted" not so much.

After my father-in-law, Norm, died, the family discussed what to put on his memorial marker. My mother-in-law, Myra, wanted to have it inscribed, "Loving Husband and Father," which is certainly an apt description. If you've spent any time looking at memorial markers in cemeteries, as I have, you know that it's also a pretty common inscription.

But Norm was a special person who treated all living things with kindness and consideration. When Norm graduated from grade school, his father wrote an inspirational note to his son in an autograph book that Norm kept on display in his office as a constant reminder of right conduct.

His father's wise words were: "Be good to yourself, and be good to humanity." We decided to put this bit of advice on his tombstone, to benefit everyone in this world who might wander by in the cemetery. Take some time to think about what you'd want to convey as your final words of wisdom for the ages.

Deciding on a Memorial Gathering Format

"What is traditional? What is contemporary? What is simple? Every family comes to this with a totally different perspective. Expectations are often based on the customs of those who have died, and their families, and their traditions," Glenn Taylor observed.

Will remains be intact and present or not? With a body present, it is a funeral, and you have a certain range of options. If the body is to be buried, where the burial is to take place impacts the funeral services. A local burial can mean a graveside service at its most simple, and the options grow from there.

The family can hold visitation at the funeral home, a chance for family and friends to see the deceased one last time (if that was his or her wish or the family's tradition), or just visit with the family before the funeral. The funeral can take place in a house of worship with a religious funeral, at a funeral home (either with a religious ceremony or not), or even at your own home, followed by burial at a cemetery.

Other religious rituals can take place with the body present, such as the Catholic rosary service, separate from a funeral mass. There is an overview of funeral services and traditions for a range of religions in Chapter Seven, "Amazing Grace."

If the deceased finished his life in Florida but has a burial plot on Long Island, he'll need to be shipped, and that's going to impact funeral arrangements. For information on shipping bodies, both domestically and internationally, see Chapter Ten, "What-If Questions."

One option is to have a funeral with friends and family in the city where the person dies, then have a graveside service at the destination cemetery. Another option is a funeral in the distant city, then a memorial service in the city where the person had most recently lived and died. Graveside services might not be advisable if the funeral is in a northern US state in the winter.

Memorial services, a term sometimes used interchangeably with funerals, are usually held without a body present, either because of cremation, body donation to science, or other reasons. Because the event does not need to be held within days of the person's death, a memorial service opens up a whole range of creative possibilities. It can be scheduled weeks or even months later. To reap the healing benefits of holding a memorial service, you may want to do the event within the first few weeks of the death, when grief is still fresh and the act of creating a service can help process mourning.

Other Details to be Determined

Among the many services funeral directors can provide is expertise in crafting a meaningful farewell and ideas for involving the entire family and other participants. They can assist with writing and submitting obituaries, receive flower deliveries and transport bouquets, request military funeral honors, obtain death certificates, and prepare memorial booklets for distribution at the funeral or memorial service.

Communications and Memorial Booklets

Obituaries that funeral directors place on behalf of the family are different from the news stories that appear for someone famous or notable in some way. These paid placements in the local newspaper can be short, with just basic information about the deceased and the funeral or memorial service, or a long recitation of the deceased's attributes and personal history.

I've often heard life history obituaries read at funerals or memorial services. Just remember, newspapers charge by the line, so the more you say, the more you pay. We'll discuss obituaries in more detail in Chapter Five, "I Have Some Sad News."

Do you want people to send flowers, or would you rather they make memorial contributions to a worthy cause? That preference can be stated in the obituary as, "In lieu of flowers, the family requests donations be made to..." or "Memorial contributions may be made to..." Beneficiary organizations usually reflect the interests of the deceased or the disease that led to the death. The funeral director will help handle flower deliveries and displays.

The funeral director can also help prepare memorial cards or programs to be distributed at the funeral. These programs often include the deceased's name, date of birth and death, speakers for the event, pallbearers, and a prayer or poem. A photo of the person may be featured.

Programs offer creative opportunities for personalization, to be explored more fully in Chapter Four, "It's My Party and I'll Die If I Want To." Many funeral homes offer memorial card printing packages that include thank you notes and a guest sign-in book.

Military and Veterans Affairs

The funeral director can help American veterans and their families obtain free services from the government. In addition to burial in any of the Department of Veterans Affairs' (VA) 128 national cemeteries with available space, the VA provides opening and closing of the grave, perpetual care, a government headstone or marker, a burial flag, and a Presidential Memorial Certificate, at no cost to the family.

Veterans who are buried in a private cemetery receive the same benefits, minus those related to interment and gravesite maintenance. Copies of the veteran's discharge papers are required to obtain these services.

Those eligible for military funeral honors are active, reserve, or former military members who departed the service under conditions other than dishonorable. The Department of Defense is responsible for providing military funeral honors, coordinating with funeral home personnel. The ceremony includes a detail of two or more uniformed military persons; folding and presenting the burial flag to the family; and the playing of *Taps*. You can find more details about military funerals in Chapter Seven, "Amazing Grace."

While spouses can be buried with a veteran in a national cemetery, bear in mind that due to space limitations, the bodies may be stacked within one gravesite. If that's not how you want your remains to spend eternity, consider other options.

In 2010, the VA began offering bronze medallions to affix onto privately purchased headstones or markers. The medallion depicts a three-dimensional folded flag surrounded by a laurel wreath with the veteran's branch of service displayed beneath. The medallion is offered in lieu of a traditional government headstone or marker.

The next of kin or those acting on a deceased veteran's behalf can order this burial benefit option. The VA will mail the medallion along with a kit that allows the family or staff of a private cemetery to adhere it to a headstone, marker, or niche cover.

Death Certificates

The funeral director will also order death certificates for the family. These are necessary documents for a number of important steps to be taken after the funeral. Death certificates are required for making life insurance and annuity claims, changing title on property, closing or changing bank or credit card accounts, and any number of financial transactions on behalf of the deceased. These important documents should be ordered while making other funeral arrangements, as their preparation can take two weeks or more.

In my father-in-law's case, the death certificate didn't arrive until eight weeks after he died. It should have been a straightforward process because he died in the hospital. But because he was transported back and forth between the hospital and a rehabilitation facility over seven weeks, the Office of the Medical Investigator needed to check the medical records to make sure there was no foul play involved. People went on vacation. Things just got stuck. It happens.

The family should carefully consider the number of certified copies of the death certificate to order. People with simple estates may only need a few, but those with complex financial situations and multiple accounts may need as many as two dozen. Consult with your financial advisor to get an idea of the best number to order.

While some organizations accept photocopies of the document, it's much easier to order extras than go back and obtain more originals. The cost per document varies by state.

Motorcade Escorts

When funeral planning, the funeral director will probably ask if you want a motor escort to facilitate the procession from wherever the funeral is held to the cemetery. This assumes that the funeral is not being held graveside, of course.

Local police don't escort funeral processions much anymore, unless the deceased was one of their own, a firefighter, or military personnel killed in battle. Most funeral procession escorts are now done by private motor escort services hired by the funeral home. They may look like police, with lights on their cars or motorcycles, and may even be moonlighting officers.

My advice: whatever it costs, get the escort. They help move the mourners safely on the journey to the cemetery, eliminating one more thing to worry about. They can stop traffic, if need be, and they stand guard at busy intersections to make sure the entire procession can keep rolling through even if the light changes to red.

For my father-in-law's funeral, two motorcycle escorts did a tag team routine as the motorcade moved from the synagogue to the cemetery, about a six-mile trip across town. One pulled into an intersection, got off his motorcycle, and directed traffic to stop until the full procession had moved through. The second brought up the rear, then zoomed to the front of the procession to handle traffic at the next intersection. While the motorcade had to stop at a few intersections, the escorts kept it moving smoothly and safely for the majority of the trip.

The cost to hire two motorcycle escorts in Albuquerque was about $400 in 2009. Costs for a motor escort will vary by market. Whenever the next energy crisis hits and the price of gasoline shoots up into the stratosphere, you can bet the cost of a motor escort will go up, as well.

Funeral Procession Etiquette

There's an alarming rise in traffic accidents related to funeral processions, as people ignore, or perhaps are ignorant of, funeral cortege etiquette.

If you are driving in a funeral procession, there are a few basic rules to follow. Allow the immediate family to be the first in line behind the hearse. They may be in a limousine or their own vehicles. Turn your headlights on to indicate you are part of the motorcade. Funeral directors may provide a "funeral" sign to put on your dashboard or a magnetic sign to attach to the vehicle to indicate you are part of a procession.

Remember to keep up with the procession, which will be moving relatively slowly — 30 to 40 miles per hour. Even when traveling on an interstate highway, a procession will likely go no faster than 55 mph. Stay close to the vehicle ahead to avoid people cutting into the procession.

When you encounter a funeral procession, remember that the motorcade has the right-of-way and allow it to pass. Here are a few other tips, courtesy of Funeralwise.com:

- **Do** be respectful.
- **Do** yield — once the lead car has entered traffic, such as going through an intersection, the entire procession will follow without interruption. Even if their traffic light is red and yours is green, you must stop and allow the procession to continue through the intersection until all cars in the procession have passed.
- **Do** look for the last vehicle in the procession — it typically has two or more flags and a hazard lights flashing. Once it passes by, you may resume the normal flow of traffic.
- **Don't** cut into or cut off a procession.
- **Don't** honk at a car in a funeral procession.
- **Don't** pass a funeral procession on the right side on a highway, unless the procession is in the far left lane.

Clothing the Deceased

Whether the person will be put on display or not, give some thought to the outfit that will go to the funeral home to dress the body. Would you want to bury Dad in a suit and tie, a uniform, or something that he was always seen wearing?

My father-in-law was hardly an athlete, yet my mother-in-law provided a soft cotton tracksuit. She wanted him to be comfortable. My Uncle Arthur, who had an on-court heart attack after a great game of singles, was buried in his tennis whites with the racquet that was in his hand when he died.

Perhaps Mom would prefer to be in a party dress for your last look at her. Wouldn't it be nice to know that whatever you picked out is something she'd really want to wear? You won't know until you talk about it. Then you can give the right outfit to the funeral director, who will take care of dressing and arranging the body.

Other innovative services that funeral homes may offer include housecleaning before the event, catering for post-event receptions, releasing balloons, butterflies or doves at the event, and creating photo or video montages to be played at the funeral or memorial service. They may offer products such as jewelry to hold cremated remains, memorial photo boards, and memory wristbands.

There is no law that stops those who want to make all funeral arrangements themselves from doing so. Just be aware of the many elements that need to be addressed when there's a death in the family.

Funeral director Brian Hanner cautioned, "Carrying out your own funeral arrangements is akin to building your own home. You can do it if you want to, but the outcome, which is often dependent upon the professionalism and expertise of your general contractor, will likely be different when you do it yourself."

Good funeral directors will work with you to smoothly make these arrangements and any others you may want. They recognize the family's shock and grief, and will respect your wishes.

Fifty Things That Must Be Done
When a Death Occurs
Courtesy of French Mortuary,
Albuquerque, NM

Notify:
1. The doctor
2. The funeral director
3. Cemetery or memorial park
4. The deceased's clergyperson and house of worship
5. All the relatives
6. All the friends
7. Employers
8. Organist and singer
9. Pallbearers
10. Insurance agents
11. Unions and fraternal organizations
12. Newspapers

Select:
13. A memorial marker
14. A cemetery lot
15. Casket
16. Vault or outer case
17. Clothing
18. Blanket or robe
19. Flowers
20. Music
21. Food
22. Furniture
23. Time
24. Place
25. Transportation
26. Card of thanks

In addition to:

27. Providing vital statistics about the deceased
28. Preparing and signing necessary papers
29. Providing addresses for all interested parties who must be notified
30. Answering sympathetic phone calls and messages
31. Meeting and talking with everyone about the details
32. Greeting friends and relatives who call
33. Cleaning home for visitors
34. Providing lodging for out-of-town guests
35. Planning funeral car list

And you must pay some or all of the following:

36. Doctor
37. Nurse
38. Hospital
39. Medicine and drugs
40. Clergyperson
41. Organist and singer
42. Funeral
43. Interment service
44. Cemetery lot
45. Memorial marker
46. Florist
47. Clothing
48. Transportation
49. Telephone and telegraph
50. Food

3

We Can Do That?

New trends in death care

"There's never a new fashion but it's old."
— *Geoffrey Chaucer, 1342–1400*

In many ways, death care in the twenty-first century is starting to return to nineteenth-century practices as families consider green burial and at-home death care. But there are some totally new things under the sun, such as webcasting funerals and technology that can reduce your remains to an ecologically safe liquid that you can pour onto the earth or into a favorite body of water. Let's look at a few new trends in end-of-life care and funerals.

Advance Directives

Before hospitals and nursing homes became the places most Americans draw their final breath, people died at home. There was no need for advance directives about what kind of medical treatment they wanted at the end of their life. With the medical miracles that can be worked today, individuals need to state their preferences about how far they want to go with heroic or life-sustaining measures, pain control, and who will speak on their behalf when they cannot.

These statements are made in living wills and power of attorney designations, known collectively as advance directives. If you have not drawn up at least some of these documents yet, I highly recommend you do so.

These documents will enable you to appoint a representative to speak for you when you are unable to speak yourself — for example, if you are unconscious, in a coma, or delirious. Last wills, trusts, and other important legal documents are related to the distribution of a person's assets once they die, but they do nothing to ensure that your wishes are followed in a medical setting.

End-of-life conversations are hard to start, but there are great resources to help get the ball rolling. The nonprofit organization Engage With Grace offers The One Slide Project at www.EngageWithGrace.org, where you can download one sheet that has five questions to answer:

- On a scale of 1 to 5, where do you fall on this continuum? (1 being "Let me die in my own bed, without any medical intervention," 5 being "Don't give up on me no matter what, try any proven and unproven intervention possible")
- If there were a choice, would you prefer to die at home, or in a hospital?
- Could a loved one correctly describe how you'd like to be treated in the case of a terminal illness?
- Is there someone you trust whom you've appointed to advocate on your behalf when the time is near?
- Have you completed any of the following: written a living will, appointed a healthcare power of attorney, or completed an advance directive?

The *Five Wishes* booklet, available online at www.AgingWithDignity.org, is also a good way to start the conversation about medical directives — how you want to be treated if you become seriously ill. It is written in understandable words and available in twenty-three languages. It meets the legal requirements in forty-two states — and it's useful in all fifty. *Five Wishes* lets your family and doctors know:

- Who you want to make health care decisions for you when you can't make them.
- The kind of medical treatment you do or don't want.
- How comfortable you want to be.
- How you want people to treat you.
- What you want your loved ones to know.

Just as talking about sex won't make you pregnant, talking about end-of-life issues won't make you dead. Have a conversation and make some advance directive statements!

Green Burial

The rising interest in green burial is, in fact, a return to the practices that our forebears used prior to the rise of the modern funeral industry. The movement first started in Britain as natural or woodland burials, avoiding embalming, metal caskets, and concrete burial vaults. In some green burial grounds, a tree is planted directly on top of each grave. The resulting forests look somewhat like tree farms.

The amount of resources spent on traditional funerals and the environmental impact is staggering. Mary Woodsen, a science writer for ten years at Cornell University, put together the following figures in 2002 based on information from mortuary schools and funeral directors. She believes these careful calculations provide a conservative estimate and the figures could actually be higher.

Every year, conventional burials utilize more than 827 thousand gallons of embalming fluid, eventually putting toxins and carcinogens into the earth; over 1.6 million tons of reinforced concrete for vaults; more than 90 thousand tons of steel and 27 hundred tons of copper and bronze for caskets; and 14 thousand tons of steel for underground vaults.

That's enough metal to build a Golden Gate Bridge each year, and enough concrete to build a two-lane highway from New York to Detroit, according to Joe Sehee, executive director of the Green Burial Council.

A typical flame-based cremation, which some consider environmentally friendly, can use approximately 25 therms of natural gas to generate 2.5 million BTUs to process one body. You may not be taking up space, but you will generate 532.4 pounds (242 kilograms) of CO_2 emissions in the cremation process.

Green burial fosters returning to the earth as naturally as possible and eschews embalming, sealed caskets to shield the body from the earth, and cemeteries of unnaturally sculpted acres. Providers are rising to address this interest, committed to reducing toxins, waste, and carbon emissions associated with conventional end-of-life rituals.

Green burial grounds can also serve as wildlife sanctuaries and nature preserves that restore and protect ecosystems. The Ramsey Creek Preserve in South Carolina was the first of this new type of green burial ground in the US. Founded in 1998 by Billy and Kimberly Campbell, at Ramsey Creek, the graves are hand-dug, shrouds or plain wooden boxes are used without a vault or grave liner, and natural stones mark the final resting places of the dead.

The Green Burial Council, a nonprofit organization, provides an eco-certification program for those in the funeral industry who wish to embrace it. As of 2010, the Green Burial Council has certified hundreds of funeral homes in forty states and three Canadian provinces.

The organization has also certified a growing number of green burial grounds around the country. When a green cemetery is operated as a nature conservancy, purchasing a burial plot can be treated as a tax-deductible contribution.

Sehee said, "We're trying to reduce the use of toxins, waste, and CO_2 emissions in death care, and involve burial as a legitimate conservation tool. We want to make burial sustainable for the planet, meaningful for the family, and economically viable for the provider."

He speaks to funeral directors around the country on the growing trend. "We have a one hundred percent voluntary market-based mechanism, and so far, so good," said Sehee. "We've harnessed a lot of consumer demand, created awareness for this idea, and now, we can leverage that by getting funeral homes and cemeteries to get on board, which we're doing increasingly."

The skyrocketing use of cremation for body disposal was a disruptive innovation in the staid funeral home industry, historically slow to embrace changes in their business model. Many funeral homes lost business to cremation providers. Green burial is a second disruptive innovation.

Sehee tells funeral directors to pay attention and respond, saying, "I tell them, you want this to be Cremation Round Two? Go ahead — diminish it, and don't embrace it. Let others provide it, because that's what will happen."

"My feeling is the real driver is connected to spiritual issues," Sehee opined. "It's innate for us to want to befriend our death to a certain degree. Cultures all over the world have done this. It's only been in the last hundred years that this idea has been co-opted from us through practices and products that impede the process of decomposition. I personally think our culture's inclination to deny death is more associated with some of the ickier aspects of conventional death care that you don't want to think about."

"Consumers should know that they do have options, no matter what end-of-life ritual or disposition choice appeals to them," concluded Sehee. "And they can find providers who will accommodate them — that's going to be increasingly easier to do."

If you've got the acreage to allow for a family plot on the "back 40," burying a body at home can also be a green burial option. Home burial options can be limited by local zoning ordinances, water table restrictions, or flowing water on the property.

Keep in mind that perpetual care of the burial site will be a responsibility handed down through the generations, and a family plot can become a liability if you sell the property. The presence of a burial site must be made known before the land is sold, and that could adversely impact property value.

Home After-Death Care

Elizabeth Knox is not afraid to look death in the face. The founder of Crossings: Caring for Our Own at Death has done it regularly since the first time in 1995, when her seven-year-old daughter died after an automobile airbag mishap.

The hospital staff told her that the body could only be released to a funeral home. Knox wanted to care for her daughter's body at her own home before final disposition. Told it was against the law (it isn't), she found a funeral home that would pick up the body and deliver it to her home. She bathed and dressed her daughter. And then family and friends shared the grief of her passing for three days before releasing the body.

Some have called her a death midwife, a home funeral guide, a funeral rights educator. Knox helps people return the final preparations of a loved one's body back into the home, as it was before the twentieth century and the rise of the funeral industry.

"This is the way we cared for our departed throughout millennia, up until about seventy-five years ago," said Knox. "The new phenomenon is having a funeral director take care of the funerals, instead of the family."

As baby boomers age and see their parents and contemporaries dying in greater numbers, she sees an increased interest in taking back the last rites of preparing a body at home. "These are the same people who took back birthing at home, or wrote their own marriage vows, or just tried to take a generalized form and make it more personal to them," said Knox.

Knox educates families on how to renew simplicity and sanctity in home death care, while retaining some control over what is done with the remains of a loved one before final disposition with burial or cremation. She addresses people's fears and hesitations about handling the dead, provides examples of at-home death care experiences, discusses state-specific laws and how to work within them, body care of the departed, and how to maintain a relationship with those who have crossed over.

"People have concerns like: What will the neighbors think? What about smells? What about fluids?" Knox elaborated. "Not once has anyone found it too much to do. If they wanted to do it, they found a way. I offer what served me in my situation and other things for them to consider. I give them freedom to find what works for them."

That includes the freedom to work with a funeral director to some degree. A family can utilize their services for transportation, cremation, and purchasing a casket, among other things. Families can choose to do the majority of after-death care activities themselves in most states, except for Connecticut, Delaware, Indiana, Nebraska, and New York.

One of the biggest misconceptions Knox regularly has to address is letting people know there are no laws that require embalming.

"So many people are selecting embalming without having a single clue of what they're choosing. If they had any idea, they would really think twice about it," said Knox. "Embalming is about the only thing funeral directors can do that we can't do, and you don't want it anyway."

However, most state laws require refrigeration of a body within twenty-four hours to delay the effects of decomposition. Dry ice arranged around a body is a very effective refrigerant but it can freeze a body solid if not used carefully. And extreme care must be taken to provide plenty of fresh air in the room. Dry ice is a solid form of carbon dioxide, and without adequate ventilation it can cause asphyxiation as the dry ice evaporates.

"Because I've been around death as much as I have, I'm not as afraid of it as many people are," Knox explained. "It's a really rewarding experience to be able to help people in this state of tremendous distress and bring them some comfort."

"If you just let love be your guide, and you have a little bit of common sense, it's not very difficult," Knox said. "It sounds scary, but if you can just feel your fear and do it anyway, you'll be amazed at the comfort and healing that it brings."

A New Eco-Friendly Disposal Method

While not in widespread use by funeral homes yet, there's a relatively new process that liquefies the body into a coffee-colored sterile solution that can be safely disposed of in water or on land without concern about toxic chemicals.

This developing green alternative to burial and cremation accelerates natural decomposition. It has different names given by four different providers: BioSAFE Engineering calls it Water Resolution®, Eco-Green Cremation System calls it Natural Cremation, Matthews International, Inc. calls it Bio-cremation or Resomation®, and CycledLife calls it by its official name, alkaline hydrolysis.

The body is placed in a specialized tank that is filled with a strong alkali solution that is brought up to high temperature and pressure. The tissue dissolves into basic life-building blocks of amino acids, peptides, sugars, and soap (actually, the salts of fatty acids), leaving white, brittle skeletal remains that are easily powdered to ash. These sterile "bone shadows" can be returned as ashes if the family desires.

The process neutralizes embalming fluid, drugs, and the body's DNA/RNA and it produces much less CO_2 than a cremation. Titanium medical implants can be recovered intact and perfectly usable in Third World countries by organizations such as Doctors Without Borders. While not yet widely used as of 2010, the Mayo Clinic has successfully used the Water Resolution® process since 2007 to dispose of bodies donated for scientific research.

Webcasting of Funerals

You may not hesitate about recording a wedding, as it's a joyous event, but you never think about recording a funeral, where people are going to say such wonderful things about you.

A cyberfuneral provides a good reason to allow cameras to cover your big send-off.

Cyberfunerals, or the broadcast of funeral services over the Internet, is a growing phenomenon fueled by our increasingly wired society. Also known as funeralcasting or memorial webcasting, it can be shown live, accessible only to those who have a password supplied by the funeral service provider. It can also be archived for repeat viewings as part of an online memorial site.

"With a significant number of funerals, at least one person would like to be there but can't, whether from work or family obligations, geographic distance, travel costs, physical or health-related challenges, military deployment overseas, or complicated or disenfranchised relationships," said Carla Sofka, PhD, associate professor of Social Work at Siena College who studied the phenomenon.

Funeral director Brian Hanner related the story of a woman missionary who spent the majority of her life, more than sixty years, working with people in Puerto Rico. She returned to her native town of New Philadelphia, Ohio when she became ill. When she died, there were about a dozen family members in the chapel in Ohio for the funeral, and almost 200 in Puerto Rico who tuned in via webcast.

Not only did they watch, a number of people in Puerto Rico had recorded eulogies and uploaded them to YouTube the day before the funeral. Hanner played the eulogies for the family in Ohio, who did not know the people in Puerto Rico. It was their first international, interactive funeral.

"I felt it did a lot of good," said Hanner. "The people here could have very easily judged the funeral as a small funeral. But the number of people who were thinking about her and praying for her family at that time was significant, and it was brought to life because so many of them could actually participate in the funeral as well."

Savvy funeral homes are adding cyberfunerals as part of the services they offer. The funeral is held in a specially equipped chapel that has the lights, microphones, cameras, and high-speed Internet access and servers to handle the bandwidth needed. Alternatively, the family can hire their own professional webcast services to carry the funeral.

To view the cyberfuneral, a person needs a late-model computer with audio and video capabilities, a high-speed processor, and a high-speed Internet connection. If you can watch YouTube, you can watch a webcast.

Some negative aspects: While cyberfunerals provide the opportunity for people to observe, there may be less social interaction with the bereaved, and a sense of community may be lost. Some may feel the cameras are too intrusive, or the event too impersonal.

Other considerations: There are issues of signed permissions to show the people at the funeral and licensing fees to be paid for music used in the ceremony. If professional photographs or copyrighted images are used, those issues must be addressed, as well.

Yet, there are benefits that live on after the event. Sofka noted, "Kids might create a memorial website, and having an archived webcast, can hear stories and learn things they never dreamed they'd know about that loved one."

Living and Dying Large

It's no secret that 67 percent of American adults are overweight, and of those, 34 percent are obese, according to the Centers for Disease Control and Prevention. Some people are just really large or tall. These bigger bodies need bigger caskets for burial, and that has implications for boomers with bad backs who may be pallbearers.

Standard caskets are between 24 and 27 inches wide, and 78 to 80 inches long. Anything larger is considered an oversized casket, and most major casket manufacturers carry a line specifically for those massive folks who won't fit into standard sizes. The Goliath Casket Company, "Standing in the Gap for the Big and Tall," makes caskets that range from 29 to 52 inches wide, and up to eight feet long. Other casket manufacturers have also added larger product lines to address the oversize market.

Keith Davis, who runs the Goliath Casket Company in Lynn, Indiana with his wife Julane, said, "Obesity is like AIDS was twenty years ago. It is raising its ugly head and is going to be a huge problem everywhere in the United States."

He added, "The families of large people want the best service for their loved ones. It may take longer to work out a plan for an appropriate service that will honor that person's life, but it can be done."

Goliath offers some points to consider when funeral planning for "one of the bigger people."

- Let the funeral director know that your loved one is one of the bigger people.
- Sometimes special arrangements must be made to accommodate the size of the casket.
- The service may need to be moved to another location due to doorway restrictions for the size of the casket.
- You may need to think of a different method of transport that honors your loved one, because the casket may not fit into a traditional hearse.
- You may need to be prepared to buy two grave plots for this one person. Check with the funeral director and/or

the cemetery operator about preparing a correctly sized gravesite.

- If you are considering cremation, have your funeral director confirm that this option is available.

When working with a cemetery, be prepared to pay two to three times more to open a wider grave than you will pay for opening a standard sized plot. Bigger grave liners to accommodate a bigger casket will also cost considerably more.

If you are asked to be a pallbearer for "one of the bigger people," find out how the funeral director is going to help you carry out this honor without damaging any vertebrae. Between the weight of the person and the casket, you may be looking at moving 400 to 500 pounds — a quarter of a ton. Distributed among six people, that's still 66 to 83 pounds each.

In many cases, pallbearers will simply escort the casket, which is on a special gurney, out of the service, and help transfer it into whatever mode of transportation will be used. You might check if a similar arrangement can be made for transfer from the vehicle to the grave, as that's where the real heavy lifting and carrying takes place. Perhaps a graveside service is the answer, so the funeral home takes care of all the moving and positioning in advance.

Cremation Casket Trends

In the not-too-distant future, you could be cremated wrapped in banana leaves.

Between the down economy and consumers' growing desire for "green" options, changes are afoot for the manufacturers of caskets designed to be burned in a cremation retort.

"It's a changing field, and our members are responding with new products," said Mark Allen, the executive director of the

Casket and Funeral Supply Association of America, which represents suppliers to funeral homes. "Families that may not have considered cremation are looking at it now because of lower costs."

The lowest cost option is to use a cremation container — essentially a cardboard box big enough to hold a body — and not purchase a casket. A memorial service or celebration of life could be held with the cremated remains, rather than a funeral with the body present.

The rental casket has been around for at least a decade. You rent the box, which is nice enough for presentation at a funeral, and the removable liner is taken out with the body and burned in the retort. Renting is less expensive than buying.

Hybrid caskets are cremation caskets designed to burn in a retort and still be appropriate for a more traditional viewing and funeral. They are composed of wood particle pressboard with a veneer surface. It looks like solid wood but breaks down easily in the retort.

A solid wood casket is more expensive for a cremation, and takes longer to burn. Soft woods such as pine or poplar will burn better than a hardwood casket, and softwood caskets cost less.

Those who want to go green with their cremation can get a bamboo casket, a woven wicker container, or even bamboo leaves (to be wrapped around the body). But, as Allen points out, "That would still have to get the support of a funeral home or the individual crematory which can set its own standards."

"There are preconceived images of a funeral, and we want people to know there are many meaningful options out there," Allen remarked.

And remember, if you're looking to cremate one of "the bigger people," check first to see if the retort will be able to handle their size. If so, you'll still need a big enough container. A few more banana leaves may be the answer.

4

It's My Party and I'll Die If I Want To

Unique memorial ceremonies, remains disposal, and receptions

"Drink and dance and laugh and lie,
love the reeling midnight through,
for tomorrow we shall die (but alas we never do)!"
— Dorothy Parker, US author, humorist, poet, 1893–1967

The short film *Carpet Kingdom* by Michael Rochford explores themes of "playing it safe" in life versus embracing our heroic, expressive selves — and that extends to funerals and the reception afterward.

At eccentric Uncle Grover's burial, his sister announces, "Everyone is welcome to come to Grover's house for a modest post-burial soiree. We have a ham, and highballs will be served." Owen, Grover's nephew, encounters his sexy cousin who declares, "This funeral your mom's throwing is so fucking un-Grover." Owen sheepishly replies, "It's a respectable affair." "Exactly," she counters.

Uncle Grover had wanted a Viking funeral.

Usually, the last thing a bereaved family wants to do is hold a party in the midst of mourning. But when people come together as a community at a funeral or memorial service, post-service receptions are beneficial for both the family and the community, offering time for mourners to continue to meet with friends and family and receive their support. Yet, the funeral and the reception don't have to conform to ideas of what's "normal" or "respectable."

Funeral or memorial service receptions can be a celebration, not a downer. The key is to focus on the life of that person and what made them so vibrant and special.

In *Carpet Kingdom*, we find out Uncle Grover had saved his skipper's life during the Korean War, but that element of his life had faded away by the time he died. It took the actions of three wartime buddies and his nephew to bring Grover's dynamic life story to light, with a spectacular finish to his funeral.

The Memorial Party Planner

When Debbie Williams lost her best friend to cancer in 2002, she held a celebration of life event that was so meaningful, people came up to her afterward saying, "You should do this as a business!" and "Will you do my memorial service?" After she was laid off from her hotel/hospitality industry job, she pondered what would be a fulfilling work for her, did some research, and started Loving Touches Memorial Services in 2009.

She is essentially a party planner, changing a traditionally sad or somber event into a celebration of life. Co-owner Beth Kingwill brings her expertise as a creative producer of special occasion videos by making loving memory DVDs for families.

In her research before starting the business, Williams found that a majority of people who had done a funeral for a family member felt dissatisfied with how traditional funeral services had gone, and that they felt pressured in their choices, especially if they hadn't preplanned.

"The worst time in people's lives is when there's a death in the family. Holding an event that celebrates the person's life is healing and very uplifting for them," Williams said.

She sees a growing trend toward cremation, possibly reaching a fifty-fifty split with burial in the next five to ten years. Generations younger than the baby boomers are leaning toward cremation, whether due to a desire to reduce environmental impact (embalming chemicals in soil, taking up space in a cemetery, the wood, metal, stone, and cement used for burial) or reduce cost (if avoiding the use of a plot, headstone, casket, etc.).

With cremation, many options open up for a creative, meaningful memorial service. "If the body is cremated, you have all the time in the world to get the family together, to wait for nicer weather, or to secure a meaningful outdoor location. You can wait two weeks, or months, however long you need to prepare. You have options outside of a three- to five-day limit when there's a funeral with a body," explained Williams.

Her research indicated that 92 percent of the people she surveyed said that the reception was a key component of a memorial service that makes the celebration of life so special.

"It can be an afternoon tea; it could be an evening cocktail party. Think about what the venue should be as a reflection of the person — eating the food that person loved, using their favorite colors and flowers — to connect attendees to who that person was," Williams said.

In addition to planning a stellar celebration of life event, Williams can help with producing beautiful programs, video DVDs or picture montages, and mementos related to the deceased. While funeral directors view her as a competitor, she said she would like to work more closely with them and feels she can enhance their business.

She has expanded the business to include helping people memorialize their pets and preplan their own funerals.

"Everyone seems to accept that their pet is going to die, but when it comes to human beings, we don't want to accept that it will happen," Williams stated. "Preplanning allows your loved ones to move forward with the service that you have laid out in advance and relieve some of the pressure on your family during an emotional time."

Living Memorial Services

In 1998, Edward "E. B." Sugars helped pioneer living memorial services. Dying of lung cancer at the age of sixty-six, this retired Santa Rosa high school teacher had a memorial service while he was still alive.

More than 200 people attended, including members of the family, friends, and colleagues. The event included a potluck dinner that was made livelier by the festive music of a local brass band.

The concept was so unique at the time, the local news story was picked up and circulated widely by the Associated Press wire service, and a German television news crew interviewed family members, as end-of-life issues were then a big topic in Germany.

Although Sugars was weak, in a wheelchair, and breathing from a portable oxygen tank, he was able to address those gathered, and hear their tributes to him. He said he wanted his friends to know he loved them, to know that death is part of life, and not to be scared.

He said, "Death is not a big deal. We've ignored it. You live — a long time, a short time, whatever. In the end, it's like a wise old woman once told me: The only thing that's important in life is how well we lived it, how well we loved the people God sent our way."

A longtime recovering alcoholic, Sugars said he never thought he would live as long as he had. Known for his sense of humor, he lifted the shadow when the hall was silent and eyes filled with tears.

"I have been favored with a wonderful life. With a little luck, my reputation will grow and grow... Hell, in another ten years, I will have walked on water," he said.

Former students, fellow teachers, administrators, son Kirk and daughter Stephanie, and many friends in the recovery community delivered eulogies and tributes. The celebration was held on the thirty-fifth anniversary of his becoming clean and sober.

At the end of the day, Sugars said, "It's been a great three months, to know that you are fading fast and still accepting the joy of life... Nothing is ever so bad that you can't see joy in a day. I will remember this as one of the high points of my life."

The living memorial service was held Saturday afternoon, and he died peacefully early Monday morning. His son, Kirk, said that the anticipated memorial service helped keep his dad alive, with the help of the doctor who did everything possible to keep him going.

Having laughed and cried with E. B. Sugars at his living memorial service, family and friends honored his wishes by not holding any further services. His obituary invited anyone wishing to add to a book of memories, started at the celebration, to contribute their stories to pass on to his grandchildren.

What a wonderful way to leave a legacy of great memories.

A Home Celebration of Life

A brave new frontier is opening up for party planning your trip to the Great Beyond. My friends Jim and Elizabeth, who keep the cremated remains of both their mothers and Jim's father in a place of honor in their family room, pioneered their own creative end-of-life celebrations at home.

Elizabeth's mother lived in a casita behind the main house, and she died in her sleep at the age of seventy-nine. Elizabeth and Jim put together a celebration of life featuring a table full of items that reflected Mom's personality and creations.

Among the family photos and framed paintings she had done as a young woman were odd items, such as twenty pairs of cotton gloves and turbans that she was fond of wearing. Mom was a librarian during her career, and had saved numerous magazine clippings on homemaking, fertility, and other topics.

She had her idiosyncrasies, particularly regarding brushing her teeth and frequently using a fresh toothbrush. Her mother's list of activities to prepare for going to church on Sundays, broken down by the minute, included twenty minutes for toothbrushing. The buckets of more than 100 barely used brushes prompted me to ask Elizabeth if her mother had all her teeth when she died. In fact, she did.

I would have never known these things about Elizabeth's mother were it not for this memorial lifetime display. These items prompted questions from guests and stories from Elizabeth's children about grandma, which their father discreetly videotaped for a treasured family record.

We toasted grandma's memory with Irish whiskey. We wrote goodbye notes that were tossed with sprigs of cleansing rosemary and fragrant lavender into a bonfire, to send her into the afterlife with her favorite scent. We sang songs of joy and love.

Afterward, my mother-in-law said, "Don't sit *shiva* for me when I'm gone, have a party like that one!"

"There's nothing holding you back from creating your own meaningful rituals. The important part is to celebrate the life, not mourn the death," said Elizabeth. "Pull the elements together by following a trail of meaning. Just pick a place to start — a statue, a picture, something. We're culturally diverse enough right now that we don't have to use the same rituals of our village."

Party Planning After a Death

When mourning follows a nightmare of death in the family, how do you construct a party? Consider what seems right for your own situation. Influencing factors include your cultural background, financial resources, the circumstances surrounding the death, and method of disposition.

Funeral director Brian Hanner said, "I've had people say, 'When I die, throw a party.' I understand and respect that, but I think we need to do our crying before we can do our rejoicing. Trying to skip the crying isn't healthy."

"At least consider inviting the dead guy as the guest of honor. We're the first people in thousands of years who are making 'encountering the dead' optional, and we are a poorer people for it," he added.

Disposition plays a role in the timing of an event. If the death happens after a lingering illness, you may be too tired to be creative with a funeral and burial if you haven't planned ahead. And if it was a sudden death, say, from an accident or heart attack, you may be too stunned to do more than go through the motions.

Cremation followed by a memorial service can give you as much time as you need to plan a meaningful gathering. If a prompt funeral is dictated by your religion, you can always plan to hold a second celebration of life event once the mourning period is over.

Interim Recognition

If you plan to wait months before having a celebration of life with cremated remains, it's helpful to do *something* right after the death that allows the community to express their grief and support you as you adjust to your new life situation.

Consider holding an open house — just one day, no official program planned. Give your friends a chance to visit, express their condolences, bring food, share memories and stories, and look at photos and videos.

A casual gathering can be an opportunity to generate additional ideas for that creative celebration of life you plan to schedule later. Friends want to help their friends, and a casual open house opens the door to accept their assistance at a time when it is most needed.

If you don't want a house full of people and their food, especially if you are allergic or sensitive to certain foods, recognize the loss with a simple ritual, such as lighting a seven-day candle right after the death and put it next to a picture of that loved one who has died. You can ask people to make a memorial contribution to their favorite charity if you can't think of an appropriate cause to support.

Selecting a Location

It's okay to get creative with a post-funeral or memorial service reception or celebration of life! In fact, as Martha Stewart would say, "It's a good thing."

Often, a post-funeral reception will be held at the home of the bereaved or a close family member. In some cases, a reception will be held at the church, immediately following the service. Alternatively, some families opt to hold a gathering at a restaurant or at a place special to the deceased. There are pros and cons for each choice.

Home

- Pros: Accessible location, no cost, most of the items for a memorial display would be at the home of the deceased; it's convenient for family; and there are few, if any, restrictions on use.
- Cons: The house may not be in entertainment-ready condition, especially after a long illness; the family may not have the tools for entertaining; or the family prefers the home remain a private retreat.

Church

- Pros: The reception can be held there right after the funeral or memorial service, most church reception halls have all the needed equipment for entertaining, and use of the hall may be included as part of church membership or have a minimal fee.
- Cons: Use of alcohol may be prohibited, the building may not be available on certain days, and activities there will be subject to rules of the church. Another consideration: funeral attendees who go to the burial will then have to retrace their steps back to church for the reception.

Restaurant or Bar

- Pros: A restaurant or bar that was a favorite place to dine can be a nice way to reflect on the life of the deceased. With advance arrangement, a menu of the foods and drinks they loved can be prepared. All the set up, serving, and clean up is handled by the restaurant staff, allowing the family the time to focus on receiving condolences and sharing stories.
- Cons: There may be limited availability of use, either in space or time. This approach may be more expensive than hosting a reception at home, unless of course, you own the place.

Special Places

- Pros: A special place for a post-service reception or celebration of life event can be any location with great meaning, such as a favorite beach, theater, museum, art gallery, botanical garden, zoo, or public park. Being in a place where the deceased loved to be helps everyone remember that person with great clarity.
- Cons: Getting permission to use the place for a reception may take time. Bringing the accoutrements for entertaining to a remote spot can be a challenge. If outdoors, accommodations for bad weather and restrooms must be taken into consideration.

Accepting Help

When there's a death in the family, well-meaning people often call and say, "How can I help?" Give these people jobs to do! Your friends can play an important role in implementing post-service receptions, especially those to be held at home.

- **Security**: If a friend doesn't mind missing the funeral, it's a good idea to have someone at the home while the service and burial are taking place. Clever criminals read obituaries for the dates and times of services, find out where the family lives, and may commit robberies while the house is unoccupied.
- **Sorting:** Your most organized friend can accept food that arrives with the guests, write down who brought what (so you can send a thank you note later), and set out the victuals.
- **Set-up**: The easiest way to serve food and drink at a post-service reception is a help-yourself buffet. You can sketch out what types of food you want in what areas, such as main dishes on the dining room table, desserts on the sideboard, and drinks in the kitchen. Ask one or two friends to place food items in their assigned areas. The person minding the house while the funeral takes place can also set up food stations for the reception.
- **Serving**: Friends can monitor the buffet for empty dishes to be removed or refilled. They can also gather the used plates, glasses, utensils, napkins, and tidy up.

Allow yourself to accept your friends' support. If not now, when?

Paper, Plastic, or the Good Stuff?

When planning a memorable reception, the question to keep in mind is what kind of party would the deceased have liked? When I think of my dad, as long as pigs in a blanket and lots of good bread were served, he wouldn't care if china or paper plates were used. Mom on the other hand would probably like to see fruits, veggies, and other healthy stuff served on the good china.

Southern funerals are renowned for their at-home receptions that use the best silver and china, with tomato aspic, fried chicken, stuffed eggs, and other food provided by the neighbors. In *Being Dead Is No Excuse: The Official Southern Ladies Guide to Hosting the Perfect Funeral*, authors Gayden Metcalfe and Charlotte Hayes say that in the Mississippi Delta, "polishing silver is the southern lady's form of grief therapy."

If you're not a regular entertainer and flummoxed by the niceties, it's okay to go with the convenience of paper and plastic. A full list of equipment for successful entertaining is included with the planning forms in Chapter Twelve, "Just the Facts."

If cost is not a limiting factor, going with a caterer can make for a wonderful reception, with all the cooking and cleaning up after the party handled for you. Some funeral homes offer reception catering as part of their services, subcontracting out that work but still overseeing the implementation for you. It's another way funeral directors are like wedding planners for the last step in the life cycle.

Menu Selection

As a reflection of the deceased, meaningful food and drink can be a great way to celebrate his or her life. If Mom's brownies were the best, or Dad was known for his barbeque sauce, serve those items in honor of their memory. Hopefully, he or she wrote the recipe down before they died! If they're still around, get those recipes now.

Honoring cultural roots with food is another way to go, such as Italian, Chinese, French, or Irish cuisines, or Jewish deli platters. You don't have to cook — order carryout or ask your friends if they can make specific dishes for you. Or hold the reception at a restaurant that specializes in such cuisines.

Many well-meaning friends will send food to the home of the bereaved upon hearing of the death. You need to decide if you want to serve the food that is sent or save it for the family to eat after the crowds have gone.

Memorial Displays

Our stuff is a reflection of our lives, and a well-put-together tabletop display of items can tell volumes about the person. The display can be assembled at a number of venues — at visitations at a funeral home, at the memorial service, either in the service or at a reception, and at home while receiving visitors.

Include any items that have meaning and can lead to storytelling. For example, my husband and I put out these items at the reception after his father's funeral: a photo portrait of his dad, a cartoon of Dad recording dog sounds, a small set of trains, a gilded rose, plaques that honored his contributions to education, a Lipton tea bag, and pictures of the family through the years. Each item referred to a different aspect of his multidimensional life, and our friends came away with a new appreciation of his life and character.

I've seen memorial displays that included quilts, artwork and jewelry made by the deceased, woodworking tools, books, flowers, and even entire outfits on mannequins. There's a limitless range of items that can be included. Look for items frequently used by the person, things they made themselves or expressed their varied interests.

Photo and Video Montages

A number of funeral homes now offer to put together a video photomontage set to music. It can be shown at the service and used as part of a memorial display at the reception. This is also something you can do yourself.

You'll need a wide variety of images that cover the span of the person's life — plan on collecting fifty to sixty images for a four-minute presentation. A few tips for preparing a moving photomontage:

- Assemble images in chronological order, from infancy, to youth, to oldest age.
- Do not go back in time with the images once you have passed a certain stage — it interrupts the flow of the image narrative.
- Try to present a balanced number of images for each phase of life.
- Use shots that reflect the person's personality and activities — not just "standing in front of a house" images.
- Close-up shots are better than panoramic images with tiny people.
- If including end-of-life photos, be judicious — it's not their best-looking time.
- Choose a song or music that has meaning for the family or the deceased.
- Keep the presentation within five minutes — any longer, attention may wander.

When the audience is moved to tears by the end, you know you've created a loving, meaningful photomontage.

Another option, if you're thinking ahead for your own send-off, is to video record yourself giving a talk to your loved ones. Share whatever messages you'd like folks to have before you're gone. If you do create such a video, you'll need to let several folks in your family know of its existence, so they can find and incorporate it into the memorial proceedings.

Funeral "Party Favors"

A growing creative trend in funerals and memorial services is to give the attendees a special item or memento of the deceased — sort of a party favor from one's last soiree. It can be a way for the family to give away items that belonged to the deceased, as well as a way to share some wisdom of the departed with the living.

For example, after a traditional Baptist funeral for Patty Allred, a writer who was in my critique group, her family distributed copies of her self-published book, *Revelation in Pictures, Clothed with the Son*. It was a true labor of love and devotion for Patty, and there were hundreds of copies of her book in the garage.

At a living memorial service I heard about, the soon-to-be deceased, who had a substantial library, asked those who attended to take a book as a remembrance and to help clear out his abode. I also heard of a funeral where lollipops were distributed, because the woman who died gave them to everyone who came into her shop.

Memorial Programs

The memorial program is another service the funeral home can provide, but creative families can make their own programs for a memorial service. The program can become a keepsake item, incorporating more than just the order of service and participants. Programs can include poetry and writings, family history, and stories about or told by the deceased.

Another "party favor" idea is to share a favorite or secret recipe for dishes that the deceased was famous for making. These can be printed in the memorial program or on a separate card inserted in the program, or given separately to attendees.

Meaningful Music

At the service, as well as the reception afterward, music is a vital way to celebrate the life of someone who has died. iTunes and the iPod have made it easy to put together an entire soundtrack of music favored by the deceased. Or simply play the CDs, tapes, or recordings that person loved.

If he or she was musically talented, play recordings of music they created. Or pull together musician friends and have a live jam session or sing-along. If karaoke was their thing, set up the equipment for the party and have participants dedicate their selections to the deceased.

Pick music that has meaning for the family or was special to the deceased. One funeral director confided that the family of a stubborn, demanding man asked for Frank Sinatra singing "My Way" at his funeral. My brother's partner, Wes, loved New Orleans and Mardi Gras, so an upbeat, jazzy recording was played at the end of his memorial service as people left the sanctuary.

How do you choose the right songs to play? Consider the many aspects that represent the person — their family history, geographical roots, musical passions, and how old they were when they died.

At a memorial service for a young man who died at age twenty-one of testicular cancer, the gymnasium of the high school he graduated from was packed with hundreds of people.

He had prepared his own memorial service, which the program called his FUNeral.

There was a photomontage of the boy growing up, set to "Hey Ya!" by Outkast. A slower, mellower song accompanied the montage of his life as a young adult with cancer, set to acoustic guitar music that had this refrain:

"Put the keg on my coffin and think of me ever so often. Have a Loser's Day parade for all my friends. Drink up life like a river 'til the pizza man delivers. And smile and know I loved you 'til the end…"

This song is by The Push Stars, from their album *Paint The Town*. While not a traditional funeral music selection, it really worked for this young man's send-off.

Other songs that have moved me to tears at the many funerals I've attended:

- "Amazing Grace"
- "Danny Boy"
- "In My Life"
- "My Old Kentucky Home"
- "To Everything There is a Season — Turn, Turn, Turn"
- "Thank You for the Honor of Your Company"
- "Who Will Watch the Home Place"
- "You Are the Wind Beneath My Wings"

Airborne Salutes

When the spirit flies, we who remain may want to send a message to that loved one who has flown away. What better way to do so than with an aerial connection?

Why do brides and grooms use the release of doves at their wedding? I'm guessing it's to signal the start of their life's journey together. Similarly, you can use the release of a white dove at the end of a funeral to signal the spirit has flown, just like a bird, on its journey to the Great Beyond. In the warmer months, a similar effect can be achieved with a release of butterflies.

My brother's partner died rather suddenly, and many people did not have a chance to say goodbye. At the memorial service, we provided 100 white balloons tethered by a rainbow of colored ribbons. After the service, people were invited to write their goodbyes and messages for Wes on cards that were then tied to the ribbons.

When everyone had prepared their messages, we gathered outside and let them all go at once in a massive balloon launch. It was an awe-inspiring sight that lifted our spirits as high as the balloons.

Another airborne ritual involves burning things, as my friend Elizabeth did for her mother's memorial service. Burning notes to the deceased in a fire is a fine way to send your sentiments aloft. The burning of incense is a time-honored tradition in many Eastern and Western religions.

Lastly, not many folks know people who build and launch rockets, but our family has that honor. At my father-in-law's funeral, next-door neighbor John Currens volunteered to put a copy of the funeral program in the nose cone of a rocket he planned to launch. At the reception, everyone signed the program with best wishes for "Godspeed, Norm Bleicher."

The program actually got two rocket rides — one at 1,300 mph up over 3,500 feet, but the rocket caught a wind gust and was destroyed; the second was in a heavier rocket that went up over 7,000 feet at over 500 mph.

John returned the program with a note that read, "The card had quite the adventure and is in remarkable shape considering two launches, which happened to include free fall and crash from 3,500 feet. So now I return it to you with warm thoughts so it can be retired to a much easier life."

Getting Creative with Cremains

Want to have your remains shot into space like Gene Rodenberry, the creator of *Star Trek*? Prefer to compost in your own backyard garden like Lee Hayes of the folk group The Weavers? The ashes of Gonzo journalist Hunter Thompson were fired from a cannon on top a 153-foot tower of his own design, along with red, white, blue, and green fireworks.

Increasingly, the hobbies, interests, passions, and causes embraced by the deceased are reflected in how they dispose of their cremated remains.

If you love the sea, you might consider a unique green burial alternative where your ashes become part of a special reef marine habitat. If you always knew your loved one was a gem, there are companies who will turn the carbon from his or her ashes into a high-quality diamond — and you'll still have plenty of cremated remains to share in memorial jewelry, which is widely available in many different keepsake shapes and sizes.

It costs nothing for an individual to scatter cremated remains in a meaningful spot on land. It's not a problem if you own the land or get permission from a private landowner. Each state has its own regulations regarding where you can and cannot dispose of human remains.

The policies on scattering ashes in national parks, Forest Service or Bureau of Land Management land vary for individuals versus commercial scattering services. For individuals hiking into Forest Service land to scatter ashes, it's sort of a "don't ask, don't tell" policy. As long as you don't try to erect any memorials on public land, scattering cremated remains is okay; just don't do it in front of a park ranger. There are more stringent policies for commercial scattering services.

Whether the remains stay in a container when scattering ashes in a body of water depends on where and how you do it. In a relatively still setting near the water's surface, cremains can be poured into a lake or river without pieces flying all over the place.

If you are dropping them off a cliff or the side of an ocean liner (which cruise lines frown upon), it's better to keep the remains contained, so the ashes don't float into your face. Just make sure any container used for water disposal is biodegradable, such as a paper or cloth bag, and transfer the ashes out of the heavy plastic bag that contains them when returned from the crematory.

Ralph B. White was a *National Geographic* cameraman who spent his life pursuing adventure. He died in 2008 at the age of sixty-six from an aortic aneurysm.

Before he died, a friend asked White what he would want written on his tombstone. He replied that he preferred cremation and the epitaph "Ralph White is not here. He's scattered around the world."

As a member of the Adventurer's Club of Los Angeles, his buddies have carried out his wish. Carefully parceled-out plastic bags of his ashes have been scattered in the mountains of Nepal, the Australian outback, the China-Mongolian border, a Rwandan volcano, Iceland, and the waters off Zanzibar.

Someday, they'd like to get a piece of him dropped near the Titanic. White was there on the French-American expedition filming when the Titanic was found in 1985.

You may not have the inclination to be scattered far and wide like Mr. White, or have the adventurous friends to do it for you, but there are plenty of commercial resources for creative scattering of cremated remains available on the Internet.

Bear in mind, though, that some family members might want to visit at least a small part of the cremated remains of a loved one in a dedicated resting place.

Chester French Stewart, chairman of the French Family of Companies, tells the story of a young woman who flew from New York to New Mexico to visit the grave of her grandfather. However, he had been cremated and the remains scattered in the mountains with no record of the exact spot.

Stewart said, "She began weeping and said, 'How could you do such a thing as this?' We've found over the years that when people don't have a permanent place of remembrance to visit, they often regret it. While they're honoring the request of the person who died, I usually tell people it's really worth thinking about taking at least a part of the cremated remains and putting them in a permanent place to visit. Because often, it skips a generation; it's not so much the kids that are interested, but the grandkids that are trying to find their roots."

Transporting Cremated Remains on Airlines

If you plan to take cremated remains as a carry-on item, the Transportation Security Administration (TSA) offers the following guidelines.

Passengers are allowed to carry a crematory container as part of their carry-on luggage, but the container must pass through the X-ray machine. If the container is made of a material that generates an opaque image and prevents the Transportation Security Officer from clearly being able to see what is inside, then the container cannot be allowed through the security checkpoint.

Out of respect to the deceased and their family and friends, under no circumstances will an officer open the container even if the passenger requests this to be done. Documentation from the funeral home is not sufficient to carry a crematory container through security and onto a plane without screening.

You may transport the urn as checked baggage, provided that it is successfully screened. The TSA will screen the urn for explosive materials/devices using a variety of techniques; if cleared, it will be permitted as checked baggage only. Some airlines do not allow cremated remains as checked baggage so please check with your air carrier before attempting to transport a crematory container in checked baggage.

Crematory containers are made from many different types of materials, all with varying thickness. The TSA suggests that you purchase a temporary or permanent crematory container made of a lighter weight material—such as wood or plastic—that can be successfully X-rayed.

A Real Irish Wake

The Irish wake is idolized as a great way to send off a loved one. Here's some background on the practice from RootsWeb.Ancestry.com, in case you'd like to do your own variation.

The traditional Irish wake was commonplace around Ireland up until about the 1970s. This was the process of laying out the body of a departed relative in the house where they lived and perhaps also died.

All of the family and quite a few of the deceased one's neighbors and friends would gather at the house. There would be lots of food and plenty of drink to be consumed.

People came to socialize and remember the departed person's life. This wasn't a time for tears. Indeed, it was more of a party than a funeral. It was the traditional Irish way of celebrating each person's life and ensuring that they had a good send-off.

The wake is the period of time from death until the body is conveyed to the care of the church, generally the evening before the day of burial. Just to be clear, this is a Catholic religious tradition.

Steps in the Process of the Wake

1. Neighboring women experienced in laying out the body gather at the house of the deceased.
2. The body is washed.
3. A habit is put on the body.
4. A bed is prepared for the body.
5. If the deceased is male, he is clean-shaven before the habit is put on.
6. A crucifix is placed on the breast and rosary beads are put in the fingers.
7. Sheets are hung over the bed and along two or three sides.
8. Candles are lit and placed near the body.

Keening and Crying — Vocalization over the dead is very important.

1. The women who prepared the body join the family.
2. The mourning family produces either muffled sobs or loud wailing related to the depth of sorrow.
3. In the event that the death was considered a "great loss" (a parent leaving a large family or tragic or early death) keening is most intense and heartfelt.
4. After a while of keening, mourners are led away from the bedside by a few neighbors and are consoled.
5. Word is sent out to distant relatives and is spread with the help of a local shop or village.
6. Preparation and keening is not held for the arrival of others.

7. If the person dies late in the evening, the main wake is not held until the following night so as to give neighbors and distant relatives time to attend.

Preparations and Requirements for the Wake

1. Two men, a relative and a neighbor, take part.
2. The coffin is ordered (traditionally made by a local carpenter at the wake house).
3. Supplies are brought in — bread, meat, food of all kinds, whiskey, stout, wine, pipes, tobacco, and snuff. Tobacco and snuff are extremely important, as is alcohol.

Set Up of the Wake House

1. A plate of snuff is taken to all for a pinch. A clay pipe filled with tobacco is given to all and all are provided with food and drink — traditionally a meal.
2. Pipes filled with tobacco are offered.
3. The house layout determines the resting place for the corpse. A table, settle, or bed in the kitchen or another room is often used. A loft may be used.
4. The clocks are stopped as a mark of respect.
5. All mirrors are turned toward the wall or covered.

Watching the Body and Ritual of Visiting the Corpse

1. A corpse must not be left unattended for the entire wake.
2. A person, usually a woman, sits nearby.
3. On entrance, the mourner makes his or her way to the side of the corpse, kneels down, and silently recites a few prayers for the departed soul.

4. The mourner is then welcomed by the relatives and expresses sympathy. "I'm sorry for your trouble..." then the mourner speaks kindly of the deceased.
5. The mourner is offered food and drink for the hours spent at the wake. If the weather is good, the men congregate outside — if not, they go to the kitchen (this is very important and traditional). The corpse is often in the parlor and there is a division between the room of the corpse and celebration.
6. The mourner stays for a few hours. The old men and women come in the morning and, with the end of the working day, others in the community stop in.
7. The visitation lasts until midnight.
8. The rosary is recited once or twice — at midnight and then towards morning. The rosary is led by an important figure, such as a teacher or leader, who recites the first decade, then the relatives take part. A truly traditional wake will have a special rosary for the dead and traditional prayers. The rosary is said around the corpse, with those around the house reciting the responses.
9. Most visitors leave at midnight.
10. Close neighbors remain till morning. They drink tea, whiskey, or beer and talk about general affairs. Anecdotes are told with quiet laughter but within a solemn and decorous mood.
11. There are two funerals for the corpse — the first, in the evening, and the second, when the body is taken to the graveyard the next day.

Note: Sadly, this form of send-off is not practiced much anymore in Ireland, except probably in remote areas where Irish traditions are still very much alive.

Where Everybody Knows Your Name

I've been to many creative funerals and memorial services, but one celebration of life event held in a bar really stands out. The gathering was in honor of William K. "Big Bill" Baldwin, who started a number of taverns and a liquor distributorship. A celebration of life event was held at one of his properties, the Horse & Angel Tavern.

Upon arrival, I was given a Warsteiner wristband and two drink tickets. Waitresses took drink orders and brought them to visitors. Two photo boards had been set up, featuring pictures of Big Bill throughout his life.

A dozen beautiful flower arrangements that had been sent to the family were arranged along a window near Big Bill's regular table in a cozy corner of the bar. The flowers flanked a TV set showing CNBC programming. At least a dozen TV sets were going throughout the bar, all set to different cable channels for sports, comedy, and news.

Big Bill had lunch every day at the Horse & Angel Tavern. At his regular table, a plaque had been posted on the wall: For "Big Bill" 1929–2009. A RESERVED FOR PRIVATE PARTY sign on the table kept the space open for family.

There, I met his wife, Bettye Jo and daughter, Jill. Son Billy was all over the place, talking to many, many people, and exchanging hugs and handshakes.

There was no formal program or presentation, just lots of good conversation among people who knew the man and his family. Two large tables were laden with a buffet featuring all sorts of wonderful food, and more dishes came out of the kitchen as the event rolled on.

The bar filled up with many friends who came to wish the family well. It almost looked like a regular day in a bar, with lots of mixing and mingling. When I finally got a word with

Billy Baldwin, he told me that his father had been cremated, and the ashes would be scattered in various places that Big Bill loved, such as San Diego and Canada.

Big Bill didn't drink or smoke, so I wondered why he went into the liquor and tavern business. But he was a good man who will be missed by many, and this celebration of life event was a most appropriate send-off. His friends gathered in the spot where everybody knew his name and his nature to bid him a fond farewell.

5

I Have Some Sad News

How to handle communications

"For three days after death, hair and fingernails continue to grow, but phone calls taper off."
— *Johnny Carson (1925–2005)*

No one wants to be the bearer of sad tidings. While spreading the word about someone's death is never easy, being prepared helps make the process easier to handle. Our options for communications have evolved from telephone and newspapers to emails and Internet/online avenues. These communication vehicles have their unique requirements and rules to be effective.

Telephone Communications

The most personal way to tell family or friends that someone has died is to call them on the telephone. I know email is a very popular way to communicate these days, and using Facebook and Twitter are all the rage.

However, not everyone is online 24/7, not everyone's computer works all the time, and important people in your life may not get the message. One family friend missed my father-in-law's funeral because I had relied on email to inform a group of friends, and his computer was in the shop.

The death of a loved one is cause to pull out the entire phone list of family and friends and start calling. If a family member or friend has asked how they can be of assistance, putting them to work making these telephone calls can be a great service for a grieving family.

What to say when you call: If you get an answering machine, leave a message with just the facts — so-and-so has died, the funeral or memorial service will be at this date, time and place, there will be a gathering afterward at such-and-such a place, and if you want more information, call me back at this phone number. Repeat the number so the person can make sure they get it right.

If you get a live person on the phone, it helps to be prepared with answers to possible questions. They may want to know more about how old the person was and how they died, how the spouse or family is taking it, and other details about the person's last days. Some may ask how they can be of assistance.

Be prepared to say if flowers are welcomed and where they should be sent, or if a memorial contribution is preferred, what organization should be contacted and how. If someone wants to provide food for the family, know when and where dishes can be delivered and if there are any allergies or preferences that need to be accommodated.

Email and Online Contacts

Email is helpful for keeping large groups of friends and relatives informed and updated during a loved one's illness. However, as noted earlier, it has its drawbacks for funeral announcements, such as malfunctioning computers, or the address you've been using for a friend is no longer their primary account and the note is ignored for days.

There are different ways to utilize email to inform and invite people. You can send individual notes, one person at a time, and although it can be time-consuming, you can personalize each note. It's quicker to email groups of people within your email address book, but a bit less personal.

You can also use email services, such as Constant Contact or E-vite, to send out professional-looking announcements. However, you will need to input email lists if you don't have an account set up yet.

Another advantage to using these services is the ability to tell who opened the email, so you can make a phone call to those who haven't seen the note. This way, no one misses the event because they didn't see the information.

An email funeral announcement is much like any other event invitation, including date, time, and place. You might also include information about memorial contributions and other details about the memorial service. Here's a made-up example:

Dear Family and Friends:

I'm sad to inform you that Samuel Clemens died of a heart attack on April 21 at the age of 74. While he was known for the quip "The report of my death was an exaggeration," this time we're not kidding. We will miss his terrific wit and storytelling.

The funeral will be held on (day, date, month) at (time) in (place and address). Burial will follow at (cemetery name and address). Please join us at home afterward for refreshments and reminiscing. The address is (street address and city).

If you will be traveling from out of town, we have arranged discounted room rates at the Mark Twain Hotel, (address and phone number). Let the management know you are with the Clemens party.

In lieu of flowers, please make a memorial contribution in Samuel Clemens' name to (organization, address, phone number, website). If you have any questions, feel free to call me at (number) or (alternative contact name and phone number).

Remembering Samuel Clemens with love,
Gail Rubin

Facebook has developed into another online communications vehicle to convey this kind of news to family and friends. Etiquette columnist Thelma Domenici addressed the idea of using Facebook to extend condolences in her weekly column in the *Albuquerque Journal*, saying it's an appropriate medium.

She gave the example of a friend whose mother recently died, and how Facebook became a source of comfort as she received support from her extended circle of family and friends through the social networking website. Through Facebook, she both shared the sad news and received messages from longtime and faraway friends, who shared beautiful memories that may not have surfaced otherwise.

"I don't think a computer message can delete the need for direct contact," said Domenici. "When someone suffers a great loss, friends and family should do all they can and be as physically present for that person as possible. Cards, calls, visits, and the presence of family and friends at the funeral service were still of vital importance to my friend's healing, but Facebook had its place, too."

She continued, "So while you shouldn't use Facebook to avoid other contact that the person needs from you, don't be worried that your kind sentiments left there won't be appreciated or will be frowned upon. I'd also suggest that you make sure the person is active on the Facebook site during his trials, as you wouldn't want your message to go unread. Technology does have a heart — it's yours."

Obituaries

The reading of newspapers is declining as the population ages and dies. The old joke goes, "If I read the obituaries in the morning and I'm not among those listed, I must be alive and can go about my day."

There are two primary types of obituary stories that you see in the newspaper: news articles written about someone famous or remarkable in some way, and paid obituaries that a family places in the section of the newspaper devoted to those listings... kind of like the classified ads of death.

News Obituaries

News obituaries, or "obits" for short, are mini-biographies that focus on the person's life and times and the contributions they made. If done well, you'll learn something not commonly known. Obits originated as death notices that evolved with writers interviewing family and friends. These stories may not necessarily please the family, since a news story may reveal the deceased "warts and all."

News obituary writing is an art form and, depending on the size of the newspaper, can be a category within a newspaper's staff. A dead celebrity's story can appear anywhere in the paper, not just on the obituary page. Michael Jackson's death at the age of fifty was on the front page in many papers, and the media circus around his demise and the funeral kept the story alive for months.

When author and Oscar-winning screenplay writer Budd Schulberg died at the age of ninety-five, the *New York Times* did an article about him in the Sports section. Schulberg, who wrote *On the Waterfront*, which had that famous scene with Marlon Brando declaring, "I coulda been a contender," had a passion for boxing throughout his career.

You don't have to be famous to get news articles written about a loved one. My brother's partner, Wes Vincent, founded the Blue Eagle Book Shoppe, a noted Albuquerque metaphysical emporium with books and items to help spiritual seekers of all kinds.

When Wes died, I contacted the two local daily papers and let them know a bit about Wes and the shop, sent in a nice photo, and provided contacts of people to interview. The stories ran prior to the memorial service with details for those who wanted to attend.

In general, the best people to contact for a news obit are either the paper's regular obituary writer or a metro/local news page editor. At bigger newspapers, there may be an editor just for obits. Depending on what your loved one was noted for, and the size of your local newspaper, you might contact the arts editor/writer for an artist, the sports editor for an athlete, the business editor for a local businessperson, and so forth.

Another option for a news obituary is trade publications. My uncle, Arthur Cohen, was a big tennis fan, both playing the game and collecting memorabilia. A founding member of the Tennis Collectors of America, he collapsed and died on the tennis court after playing a great game of singles and just starting a round of doubles.

In addition to writing a paid obituary to run in *The Washington Post*, the family's local paper, I contacted the editor of *Tennis Week* magazine with the obit information. The editor asked for more details, and I sent my eulogy for the funeral along with other information about the "tennis museum" in his home. From those emails, the editor prepared an article that ran in the online version of the publication.

Classified Obituary Listings

The newspaper reporting staff has nothing to do with the classified obituary listings, which the family pays for. "It's just like a garage sale notice that comes from the funeral home or the family," said Carolyn Gilbert, founder of the International Association of Obituarists, an organization of professional obituary writers.

"The classified obituaries are not fact-checked, but taken as presented with no professional writer involved," Gilbert explained.

"So many people don't have a clue about how the obituary actually appears. They kind of think that you die and God writes you an obituary and it gets in the newspaper," said Gilbert.

"They just don't realize that there is a process and if that process is left to chance then, it is often written by a family member who is in terrible grief and has lots of decisions to make, or a funeral home person who's filling in the blanks."

It's important to think in advance about what you want said in your obituary and write something down. "People want to avoid thinking about dying, except for the terribly maudlin people who think about it all the time, but most of us do not want to think about it. That's why people put off doing their funeral plans and what's going to be in the newspaper about them," said Gilbert.

So, how can adult children extract information from their parents while they're still able to convey stories? It can be difficult to get all the details right in a short period of time. You might sit down with them and fill out the Obit News Bits Form in Chapter Twelve, "Just the Facts." It provides a place to collect details about schooling, work, interests, membership in organizations, hobbies, military service, etc.

Getting information about these areas can also guide you toward individuals who may want to know about the death in the family whom you may not automatically think to call. You don't need to use all the information collected, but it's better to have it than not.

Funeral director Brian Hanner, in his Ask the Director blog, suggests asking the following questions to prepare a good obituary and frame a life story about the person who has died:

- Where was your loved one born? In addition to providing a helpful detail in an obituary, this information is required for death certificates in most states.

- Was his or her birth order of significance? The oldest of ten children usually is a talented caregiver. The presence of siblings during rearing often defines our role in society.

- Where did he/she receive their education? The answer to this question might not be at a school! Usually listing any educational and professional degree earned is important.

- What special hobbies and interests did that person have early in life? These can lead to the development of lifelong passions, a career, or cause.

- Were there moments of importance in church, fraternal or civic life that are worthy of note?

- Are there mentors that the deceased spoke of during his/her lifetime?

- How were special relationships created? How did the deceased meet his/her spouse?

- Who are the family members to list? These are usually parents, siblings, children, grandchildren, great-grandchildren, and occasionally, special nieces and nephews, close friends, and caregivers.

- Did the deceased have special talents or gifts that will be missed?

- Are there words of wisdom (printable or otherwise) that you can imagine your loved one relaying?

Hanner noted, "Death itself is not a tragedy, in fact, it is a certainty for all of us. Being forgotten, however, is a tragedy that a carefully planned obituary can help all of us to avoid. How will the legacy of the person who died be defined?"

You can also write your own obit and instruct your loved ones to run it when the time comes. But, as Carolyn Gilbert pointed out, most folks don't want to think about their own death.

My father-in-law, Norm, fully intended to write his own obituary, but somehow never got around to it. The family opted to run a very basic newspaper obit prepared by the funeral director and left the specifics of his life to be spoken during the eulogies at the funeral. This was what ran in *The Albuquerque Journal*:

Norman Bleicher, 82, a resident of Albuquerque since 1995, died Tuesday, April 14, 2009. He is survived by his wife of 59 years, Myra Bleicher; son, David Bleicher and wife, Gail Rubin; son, Steven Bleicher and wife, Helaine Cohn; and brother, Philip Bleicher and wife, Juanita. He will also be missed by many friends. Services will be held on Thursday, April 16, 2009, 10:00 a.m., at Congregation Albert, 3800 Louisiana Blvd. NE. Interment will follow at Fairview Memorial Park, 700 Yale Blvd. SE.

Memorial contributions should be made to the Jane Goodall Institute, 4245 North Fairfax Drive, Suite 600, Arlington, VA 22203 or give@janegoodall.org. Please visit our online guestbook for Norman at RememberTheirStory.com. French, 111 University Blvd. NE, 505-843-6333

This obituary was simple and straight to the point. When death is preceded by a long illness, sometimes creativity takes a back seat to the specifics of naming family members and announcing the funeral.

My cousins asked me to help prepare an obit when Uncle Arthur died suddenly, as they considered me the writer in the family. We incorporated information about his interests and professional life in a more detailed obituary. Here's what ran in *The Washington Post*:

Arthur Steven Cohen, 75, died suddenly January 16 while playing a great game of tennis. A pharmacist who worked with Giant Food for 22 years, he was an avid player and collector of tennis memorabilia. A founding member of the Tennis Collectors of America, he belonged to the Aspen Hill Racquet Club for more than 30 years. For 20 years, his Nostalgia Ads business rescued old magazines for artwork and gifts. He leaves his loving wife of 49 years, Muriel Cohen; children Scott Cohen and wife Laura, Florence Weiner and husband Mark, Jaye Cohen and wife Stephanie. He loved teaching tennis to his grandsons Hunter, Spencer, Benjamin, and Evan. Many good friends will miss him.

Funeral services will be held Monday, January 19 at 10:30 a.m. at Temple Emmanuel, 10101 Connecticut Avenue, Kensington, MD, followed by burial in King David Cemetery, Falls Church, VA. In lieu of flowers, the family requests donations to the American Heart Association. The family will receive visitors at home Monday evening. Hines-Rinaldi Funeral Home, 301-622-2290

A paid obituary does not have to list the cause of death. Most news obits will list a cause of death, such as heart attack, cancer, stroke, an accident, etc. Remarkably, dying of old age doesn't seem to count as a cause of death.

In fact, old age cannot be listed on a death certificate as a cause of death. This adds to a general aversion to recognizing death as a natural part of the life cycle. When a story runs about someone over the age of ninety-five who has died, and no cause of death is listed, I often comment to my husband, "Gee, what do you suppose they died of?"

There is no "right" way to write a classified obituary. It can be as detailed or as brief as you wish to make it. If it is written at the time funeral arrangements are being made, most funeral directors will gladly help assemble the appropriate words for you.

Obituaries for Historical Research

Both the paid classified obituary and the free news obituary play a role beyond letting people know the time and place of the funeral or memorial service. The obit can be a valuable record for future generations to trace family history and genealogy, listing details such as mother's maiden names, names of children, grandchildren, nieces and nephews. Historians, genealogists, and social scientists also rely on obituaries to collect information.

Often, news obit stories avoid including many descendant's names, as the newspaper is providing the space for free. Of course, when listing names in a classified obituary, the more you say, the more you pay. But it may be worth the extra words for the family record of lineage.

"In a paid obituary, it does generate more words, and that turns into dollars. We are getting accustomed to reading obituaries that do not name the next generation," explained Gilbert. "If the next generation is not named, then when a family or a funeral home is following the pattern they see, they will typically not name them."

Display Advertising with Websites

Increasingly, the Internet, combined with newspaper advertising, is being used to announce memorial services for someone who has had an impact in many different cities. You may see display ads in the *New York Times* or in selected local newspapers announcing the death of a somewhat prominent person, with a photo and a bit about who they were, along with a website address. Interested people can go to the website to learn more about the person and get information about the memorial service.

With this type of communication, the event will almost always be a memorial service done without the body present, given the time it takes to determine a date, place, and time; set up a website; and arrange for the advertising. This approach also involves a lot of money, as display advertising in major newspapers is expensive, not to mention the expense of setting up a website and coordinating a large memorial service.

Online Memorial Sites

Our lives are now lived in both the real world and the virtual online world. When someone dies, their bodies are disposed of, but their online presence remains. Those Facebook profiles, Twitter feeds, blogs and other online accounts are still out there, a virtual life after death.

Facebook allows groups to set up pages and contribute postings to honor someone who has died. Each group has an officer and administrator, and friends or admirers can post comments, photos, videos, and links related to the deceased. Some of these sites have hundreds of members, others just a few dozen.

The deceased's full name, date of birth, account email addresses and other information is needed to either delete a Facebook account or change the page over to a free Facebook Memorial. Memorializing the account removes contact information, online group memberships, and personal information, such as favorites.

You can report a death and memorialize or remove Facebook profiles at this link: www.facebook.com/help/cont act.php?show_form=deceased.

Scanning these memorial pages, it appears that when someone dies, there is an outpouring of comments which tend to taper off, leaving a couple of introductory paragraphs at the top of the memorial page to introduce visitors to the deceased. There is an option for posting recent news, which would go to all the members of the group, but you know, once you're dead, you don't make much news.

Increasingly, funeral homes now provide online memorial sites as a part of the services they provide. For example, French Funerals and Cremations, which did my father-in-law's funeral, provides an online guest book called RememberTheirStory.com that they mention in the obituaries they post for clients.

In addition to running the obituary, friends and family can post condolence notes or memories of the deceased, photos can be shared as a memorial picture board, and memorial donation contact and service information is provided. This service did not cost our family any additional fee, but other funeral homes may have different arrangements.

Other funeral homes may use their online sites to minimize the cost of a classified obituary. The newspaper ad announces the person's name, age, and date of death, then keeps it short by referring readers to a web page to read the obituary. On the Internet, you're not charged by the word.

There are memorial sites not related to funeral homes that provide an Internet space for honoring a deceased loved one for a price. Some sites charge a monthly recurring fee, while some charge a one-time fee to set up a lasting online memorial. Yet others offer minimal, free memorial information as a way to get you involved, and then offer an upgrade to a paying level of service.

Just search online for memorial sites and you'll find plenty of options to choose from.

Thank You Notes

There's an alarming trend in paid newspaper obituaries — the general thank you note to the public. The family places a notice in the classified obituaries section that reads like this:

> The family of John Doe would like to thank all of their relatives and friends for the kind expression of sympathy extended to them during their bereavement (then naming specific people) Name of Funeral Home, (contact info)

Or:

> The family of Jane Doe wishes to thank their many friends and relatives who reflected on her life. Your sympathy and thoughtfulness will always be gratefully remembered and deeply appreciated. Name of Funeral Home, (contact info)

Perhaps these ads are placed as a way of thanking people who may have been inadvertently overlooked to receive a personal thank you note in the confusing days after someone has died. Part of the challenge of writing thank you notes is keeping track of what everyone did.

That's one reason for sign-in books at funerals and memorial services, so the bereaved family may know who attended and they can thank each person. It also helps to have a friend make a list to keep track of who brought food and what they actually provided.

But I don't think that's what's going on with these thank you ads. The grandmothers and great-aunts who drilled the importance of writing a personal thank you note into the psyches of the baby boomers have died. Younger generations, the text messaging crowd, know nothing about the niceties of sending a few words of thanks, and that's a shame.

Thelma Domenici, in one of her etiquette advice columns, said that a verbal thank you is fine for meals sent during a time of illness or death in the family. "I must assume that a person delivers a meal during these types of life-changing situations because they understand the recipient's need for help and time. Continue the generosity and be satisfied with a sincere verbal thank you," Domenici said.

She added, "If you are the recipient of such kindness, give the very best thank you that you can at the time. It is always gracious to send a note thanking those who were kind to you for their efforts. Your friends will be honored by it."

The writing of thank you notes can actually be a healing activity, an opportunity for grieving individuals to count their blessings. Thank each and every person who helped in whatever way they contributed with a short note, written by hand on a piece of paper.

It can be on stationery, a blank art card, a Thank You card — heck, even notebook paper works. Alright, you can send a thank you note by email to people you regularly communicate with online, but write something.

A basic thank you note expresses your gratitude for the kindnesses extended to you during this very stressful time. It can be as simple as, "Thank you for your presence at the funeral. It's comforting to have you in my life right now." You don't have to write a letter — it's a *note*. You can say plenty in three sentences.

Vary the note based on what the person did for you. Start with two sentences specific to the recipient:

"Thank you for being a pallbearer. Having you carry (name) to the grave means a lot to us."

"Thank you for the delicious casserole. It helped sustain us when none of us felt like cooking."

"Thank you for your moving words at the funeral. We will remember your tribute always."

"Thank you for your card. We were so moved by the outpouring of support we received."

"Thank you for the flowers you sent. They were so fragrant and lovely."

"Thank you for traveling here to attend the funeral. Your presence meant so much to us."

Your third sentence can be a sign-off you use for everyone:

"We are (or I am) so blessed to have you in our lives (my life)."

"Mom would have been pleased."

"Thanks again for all you did for us."

Of course, if you want to say more, feel free. It just seems that people are scared away from writing thank you notes, perhaps thinking that it requires essay-length effort.

No, when the death of a loved one blows your world apart, thank you notes are little pieces of writing that add up to a quilt of gratitude for the people in your life that come together in support.

And when you sign off, sign it "love," or "with love," no matter to whom you write. Expressions of love are what living is all about. Share the love, as it has been shared with you.

Writing Condolence Cards and Letters

Caring people call or send a card, letter, or note of condolence upon hearing news of a death. Taking time out of our busy lives to acknowledge a death and say that the person will be missed helps us better appreciate being alive.

Condolence communications need not be intimidating. Just buying a card and signing your name is easy, but not as comforting to the recipient as it could be. Adding one or two lines on what the deceased person meant to you makes all the difference in the world.

You might consider using sentences such as:

"We loved (name) and we'll miss (him/her) more than you will know."

"I always admired (his/her) (positive character attribute, such as sense of humor, generosity, knowledge)."

"(Name) was a good person and I'm so glad I had the chance to know (him/her)."

"In (name's) honor, we have made a contribution to (organization)."

A line in support of the bereaved is also appropriate:

"Please let us know if there's anything we can do to help."

"I'll be in touch in another week or so to see how you're doing."

"May I take you to lunch next week?"

Add a few additional sentences with a short story about a memory of the deceased, and you'll have a beautiful condolence letter. It doesn't matter if you write on a card, on stationery, or plain old paper.

Taking the time to write, address an envelope, and mail your communication speaks volumes. And yes, you may send an email, but remember — the family's routine has been shattered and they may not be online for a while.

A few of you may be thinking, "What if the guy who died was a jerk?" Just leave off your thoughts about the deceased, but still express your support for the family. And even if you're thinking, "Boy, I bet you're glad he's gone," refrain from saying so. Relationships are complicated, especially when someone dies.

6

Lend Me Your Ears

Writing ethical wills, eulogies and funeral oratory

"Friends, Romans, countrymen, lend me your ears!
I come to bury Caesar, not to praise him…
Bear with me; My heart is in the coffin there with Caesar,
And I must pause till it come back to me."
— *Mark Antony in* Julius Caesar
by William Shakespeare

Jerry Seinfeld joked that there's a poll that showed people fear public speaking even more than they fear death. He said, "If that's true, then at a funeral, you're better off in the coffin than doing the eulogy." I've spoken at a number of funerals and memorial services, and I can tell you, delivering the eulogy is always better than lying in the coffin.

So, let's talk about what gets said at funerals and memorial services. You have your eulogies, other spoken forms such as funeral poems or elegies, and final comments, all provided by those who knew and loved the deceased. Clergy provide homilies or sermons, benedictions, commendations, psalms, and prayers if it's a religious ceremony. With advance preparation, the dead themselves can speak at their own funeral through an ethical will.

The Ethical Will

In days of yore, the last will and testament included statements of ethics, but today's wills usually focus on the distribution of material goods the person is leaving behind. The ethical will articulates the deceased's testament, a sharing of that person's values, beliefs, wisdom, and parting thoughts that can provide moving words at a service.

The writing of ethical wills is fostered in Judaism. When adults reach the age of fifty, they are considered elders of the congregation who have enough life experiences to be able to dispense words of wisdom.

Many synagogues have a program that invites those who turn fifty to discuss Ecclesiastes, a book in the Hebrew Bible that is famous for the phrase, "To every thing there is a season, and a time for every purpose under heaven." Ecclesiastes reflects on the meaning of life and our quest for happiness. Participants also write their own ethical will and read it aloud to the congregation at a special Sabbath service.

Even if you have no children for whom to leave a legacy, writing an ethical will can help you identify what you value most. Family stories can be told so they won't be lost forever. Those you love can better understand and appreciate you. You can leave them laughing with your favorite jokes.

What to write about? Start with what you're passionate about — why you love it and what it has given or taught you. Think about how you would like to be remembered. Are you living a life that would ensure you are remembered fondly? Do you have any answers to the ultimate questions about life, the universe, and everything? (Thank you, *Hitchhiker's Guide to the Galaxy*.)

A family member or friend can read your ethical will at a funeral or memorial service, if you let your survivors know you want it so used. Or take advantage of today's video technology and be present at your own funeral by recording yourself reading your ethical will and letting the family know it's something you want shown at your funeral. Who knows, perhaps it could go viral on YouTube!

The Eulogy

If you know your Shakespeare, you comprehend how Mark Antony masterfully manipulated the funeral crowd, turning the Roman citizens against Brutus, Cassius, and the others who assassinated Caesar. Modern eulogies, however, truly honor the deceased by painting a picture that illuminates the many facets of the person's life.

I've attended many funerals and memorial services for people I never met. After most of these events, I leave with a good sense of who that person was and how they treated other people. This is a testament to the speakers, whether clergy, family, or friends, who carefully prepare their talk about the deceased.

Yet, I've also heard plenty of talks that were all about the person speaking, and only tangentially about the deceased. Beware of the use of too many words like "me," "my," and "I."

Let's make it clear — the eulogy is not about you. Your job as a speaker at a funeral is to illuminate the life and character of the deceased, and to reflect upon how their life impacted the community gathered before you to mourn that person's passing.

To create a eulogy, Bruce Kahn, retired rabbi of Temple Shalom in Chevy Chase, Maryland, said he would sit down with the family and discuss the person's life in great detail for several hours, to truly know the person. Often things would come out that most family members didn't know — both strengths and weaknesses.

A no-holds-barred discussion is a cathartic experience for the mourners, and it enabled Rabbi Kahn to be accurate in the eulogy. He would censor the material, though, saying, "I know enough to say the right things," adding, "Every eulogy I've given, the families ask for copies."

Some ideas about what to include in a eulogy are: admirable personal characteristics of the deceased; their philosophy of life; details about family, friends, their work, interests, achievements, stories, or memories; what the person's death can mean for the community; and, if appropriate, what the family's religion has to say about death.

Please, keep it brief — five to ten minutes is plenty of time to do the job. Don't go to the funeral expecting to wing it. Prepare by writing an outline before penning a speech, and rehearse what you'll say before speaking. Words written on paper may sound awkwardly different when they come out of your mouth.

Here are additional tips about eulogies from Funeralwise.com. The most meaningful eulogies:

- Are presented by those closest to the deceased.
- Include one or two stories about the deceased. Choose a funny story to start the eulogy. This will help people remember the happiness of the deceased's life. Mention something that gave the deceased pleasure, for instance, playing music or sports.
- Frequently refer to the person who has died by name.
- Mention the circumstances surrounding the death.
- Capture the deceased's important beliefs with quotes from people who were inspirational to him or her.

- List some of the accomplishments of the deceased and the differences he or she has made in the lives of others. Include the memories of many different people.
- Discuss how the deceased has affected your own life in a positive way, as well as how his death has affected you. Be honest about your feelings. An honest eulogy is always more meaningful.
- Acknowledge mourners' pain and encourage them to exhibit grief.
- Include family members who may tend to keep a low profile (i.e. gay partners, ex-spouses, stepchildren, etc.).
- Elevate the message to deepen our awareness of mortality and appreciation for life.
- Acknowledge the value of the guests' presence to family and friends.
- State that the deceased will be missed and will always be loved.

Here's a sample eulogy that I prepared and delivered at my uncle's funeral.

I'm Gail Rubin. Arthur was my uncle.

Arthur was an only child, and Aunt Muriel is my father's only sibling. I'm the only daughter with three brothers. Arthur delighted in saying I was his favorite niece, followed quickly by saying I was his only niece. But he loved my cousins on my mother's side of the family, as well.

Arthur lived life with great enthusiasm. He, as we all know, had a passion for tennis, both playing the game and collecting memorabilia. If you come to the house later today, you can tour his tennis museum that fills two bedrooms upstairs. Once the kids left home, there was no going back, as Arthur had filled their rooms with racquets and magazines and promotional items. Sorry, kids.

He loved going to yard sales and estate sales, and getting a great deal on Life *magazines and all the stuff that became merchandise for his Nostalgia Ads business. He was a great mentor for my brother Mitch, who runs a shop in Albuquerque, New Mexico, where we both live. Mitch said that Arthur gave him three ideals: work hard, play hard, and at least once in your lifetime, own a convertible.*

Jewish tradition for burial is to place the body in a plain soft wood casket, dressed in white linen or cotton clothing reminiscent of the attire of the high priests. This combination of flesh, wood, and cloth deteriorates at the same rate, allowing a graceful return to the earth, ashes to ashes, dust to dust. It also shows how in death, we are all the same, whether rich or poor in life, and we are all high priests.

We also don't put the body on display, as that is considered disrespectful of the earthly vessel that contained the human spirit. What you can't see is that Arthur is being buried in his tennis whites, with his size thirteen court shoes, and tennis team jacket, along with the racquet he had in his hand when he died. The family felt he would have wanted it that way.

With Arthur's sudden death on Friday, we had a hard time getting in touch with my parents, who were on a cruise until Saturday morning. Arthur is the first of our parents' generation to pass on, and that's hard to accept.

I like to think that Arthur has gone on a cruise, and is temporarily out of touch. When it's our time to take that cruise to the Great Beyond, Arthur and those we have loved in our lifetimes will be there to greet us when we board. In the meantime, he'll be playing tennis on the athletic deck court, and enjoying his naps after a hard workout. May he rest in peace.

Other Oratory Forms

In addition to eulogies, funerals or memorial services may include funeral poems or elegy, final comments, and psalms and sermons at religious end-of-life events.

Funeral poems, also known as elegies, bring a dramatic level of oratory to a memorial service. The elegy began in ancient Greece as a sad song lamenting love and death. Some funeral poems express sorrow and search for consolation, while others meditate on loss, grief, death, and mortality. Famous and powerful elegy poems include:

- "Funeral Blues" by W. H. Auden
- "To the Dead" by Frank Bidart
- "Fugue of Death" by Paul Celan
- "Because I Could Not Stop for Death" by Emily Dickinson
- "Dying Away" by William Meredith
- "To an Athlete Dying Young" by A. E. Housman
- "Death Stands Above Me" by Walter Savage Landor
- "The Reaper and the Flowers" by Henry Wadsworth Longfellow
- "For the Union Dead" by Robert Lowell
- "Dirge without Music" by Edna St. Vincent Millay
- "Elegy for Jane" by Theodore Roethke
- "November" by Edmund Spenser
- "Question" by May Swenson
- "In Memoriam" by Lord Alfred Tennyson
- "A Refusal to Mourn the Death, by Fire, of a Child in London" by Dylan Thomas
- "O Captain! My Captain!" by Walt Whitman

Final comments allow an informal voicing of thoughts by those attending a funeral or memorial service. People may stand and say a few words, usually from their seats, rather than going to the front of the room.

It's best to be brief, limiting speaking to one or two minutes. As with a eulogy, these comments generally reflect what qualities you admired in the deceased, what the person meant to you, and that you will miss him or her.

Sermons and the Psalmist's Contribution

At religious funerals or memorial services, clergy may include a sermon or homily that ties the life of the deceased to tenets of the religion. Family can help clergy prepare a good sermon by sharing information on any favorite prayers, psalms, or biblical passages favored by the deceased. The Bible's Old and New Testaments contain a wealth of passages and quotes appropriate for funeral sermons, reflecting on life, death, faith, and life beyond this world.

There are a number of psalms that provide comfort at a funeral, including Psalm 25 (To you, O Lord, I lift my soul...), Psalm 27 (The Lord is my light and my salvation...), Psalm 42 (Like a deer that longs for running streams, my soul longs for you, my God...), Psalm 121 (I lift up my eyes to the mountains...), and Psalm 130 (With the Lord there is mercy and fullness of redemption...). But the one most utilized by far is Psalm 23.

The Twenty-Third Psalm

Psalm 23 is a popular reading at both Jewish and Christian funerals. It affirms that though we face trials in life, with God's support, we move through the dark times and can achieve wholeness and fulfillment.

Newer translations of this beautiful psalm have appeared in the last few decades. The version that follows is the traditional King James translation that includes the somewhat awkward "est" endings to verbs. If you prefer to use gender neutral names, you can replace "The Lord" and "He" with "God," "The Divine," or the Hebrew name "Adonai."

A psalm of David:
The Lord is my shepherd; I shall not want.
He makes me to lie down in green pastures,
He leads me beside the still waters.
He restores my soul.
He guides me in straight paths for His Name's sake.
Yea, though I walk through the valley of the shadow of death,
I will fear no evil
For Thou art with me.
Thy rod and Thy staff, they comfort me.
Thou preparest a table before me in the presence of mine enemies.
Thou annointest my head with oil,
My cup runneth over.
Surely goodness and mercy shall follow me all the days of my life,
And I shall dwell in the House of the Lord forever.

So many times, I've heard people speaking at funerals say, "I wish I could have told him (or her) that I loved him one more time." Remember to tell the ones you love that you do love them as often as you can. You never know when that last time will be.

7

Amazing Grace

Religious customs for death

"Say nothing of my religion. It is known to God and myself alone.
Its evidence before the world is to be sought in my life:
if it has been honest and dutiful to society
the religion which has
regulated it cannot be a bad one."
— Thomas Jefferson, third US President (1743–1826)

Couples from different faith backgrounds often face hurdles when they marry, as I know from my first marriage — a Jew to a Catholic. Clergy may try to counsel the couple on how they can bring their different religions together into their enjoined lives, or the pair may walk away from their religions altogether. Or they may find a happy medium for celebrating holidays and raising children.

At the end of life, though, religion often becomes important once again. With a death in the family, you may feel drawn to have a funeral service in the religion you grew up with, even if you haven't practiced that faith or attended services in years.

This is a hard time to learn about a partner's religious traditions for funerals for the first time. Discussing what kind, if any, religious ceremony you would want before there's a death in the family is important for reducing stress on top of grief.

"I have noticed that when a death occurs, people become more orthodox, and that's true whether it's in the Jewish faith or any other faith," said funeral director Glenn Taylor.

A late "return to the fold" for a funeral holds pitfalls for making a meaningful end-of-life ritual. If you haven't regularly attended a church or synagogue, it's hard to get a clergy person who knows the deceased personally. There's nothing sadder than attending a funeral where the officiating clergy mispronounces the deceased's name and only recites information that appears in the obituary.

Just like in art, you need to know the rules in order to break them. Options for nonreligious funerals and memorial services abound. (See Chapter Four, "It's My Party and I'll Die If I Want To.") This chapter, however, looks at various religious practices related to death, funerals, and mourning, so you may know what to expect when called upon to attend or prepare an end-of-life event for someone from a faith tradition different from your own.

Bear in mind that every family's interpretation of a funeral tradition is different. Each family will have its own unique variations regarding treatment of the body, funeral services, and mourning. When making plans within an interfaith family, it may be helpful to say, "I understand your faith tradition calls for such-and-such to be done. Is this something you want to do?"

The Pew Forum on Religion and Public Life released a survey based on 2007 information that found 28 percent of American adults have left the faith in which they were raised in favor of another religion or no religion at all.

Those who are unaffiliated — the atheist, agnostic, or "nothing in particular" — make up 16.1 percent of the population. Those affiliated with religions other than Christianity make up 4.7 percent of the population, including

Jews, Buddhists, Muslims, Hindus, Unitarian Universalists, and Native Americans.

Among all adults in the US, Christian denominations make up 78 percent of those who claimed a religious affiliation. This includes Protestant (including evangelical, mainline, and historically black churches), Catholic, Mormon, Jehovah's Witness, Orthodox (Antiochian, Carpatho-Russian, Greek, Romanian, Russian, Serbian, and Ukranian), and other Christian denominations.

Despite the diversity of doctrines within Christian churches, many of the funeral and mourning practices for this majority religion are similar. The following template outlines Christian practices in general. Later we'll look at specific practices for particular churches that vary from this form and cover rituals and customs for other religious traditions.

Appropriate funeral attire for guests at most religious ceremonies is modest and in somber, dark colors, unless otherwise noted for each religion. Men wear a suit or sport jacket and tie. Women may wear a dress, a skirt and blouse, or nice top with dress pants and jacket. Children should be dressed up as for a special family event.

Christian Denominations

Treatment of the Body: The body is usually viewed, either at a visitation event or "wake" at the funeral home and/or before or after the funeral. Wakes can last from several hours to several days. The casket is usually closed during the funeral service. Cremation, embalming, and medical donation of the body are all generally accepted.

Funeral or Memorial Services: Funerals usually take place within two or three days, or up to one week after death. The service may be held in a church or funeral home and typically last about thirty to sixty minutes. The funeral usually includes singing or music, scripture reading, prayers, a homily or short sermon, and eulogies.

A pastor or priest leads the service. Musicians can range from an organist to singers with accompanists. Family or friends may deliver eulogies or remembrances, depending on whether the funeral rites are part of a special version of the regular liturgical prayer or a separate funeral ceremony. If the body has been donated to science or cremated prior to a funeral ritual, a memorial service or celebration of life event is held without the body.

Written Material: A program with the order of the ceremony is usually distributed to guests. The program may be expanded to include poetry, psalms, an obituary, and other information. Readings from the Bible's Old and New Testaments, including selected psalms, and hymnals may be used.

Do's and Don'ts: Sign the guest book. Usually, ushers will advise where to sit. In some denominations, you may seat yourself where you wish. If you arrive late, do not enter when the bereaved family is entering or during prayers. Taking pictures or recording the service (both audio and video) is generally prohibited, but this can vary with each church. Check with the pastor before using such equipment during a service.

It is usually optional for guests of other faiths to kneel, read prayers aloud and sing with the congregation, but it's good form to stand when others stand up. When viewing the body, which is optional, approach and observe silently and somberly. Express your condolences to the family after the service. It is appropriate to visit the bereaved at home after the funeral, depending on how close a relationship you have.

Interment: Attending the interment ceremony can be optional for some denominations. Most guests should attend, unless the interment is private. At graveside, the service may include Scripture reading, prayers, songs, and committing the body to the ground. Some denominations ask attendees to sprinkle earth on the casket in the grave.

Post-Event Reception: Guests may visit the bereaved at home after the funeral, or there may be a reception at the church or a restaurant. Length of time for the visit can vary from thirty minutes to several hours. Food may be served, and in some homes, grace will be recited first. Some denominations will not serve alcoholic beverages. Religious services are rarely, if ever, held in the home.

Gifts and Cards: Upon learning about the death, telephone, send a card, or visit the bereaved to offer condolences, sympathies, concern, and assistance. It is usually appropriate to send flowers to the home or funeral home prior to the funeral. The family may suggest memorial contributions be made in lieu of flowers. Sending food before or after the funeral is usually appropriate, as well.

Mourning Period: There is no official church doctrine regarding how long a mourner stays away from work or socializing. A mourner might return to work after a few days or a week or two. They may return to a normal social schedule within two months, but it depends upon the individual. In many cases, the individual and local cultural traditions determine when a mourner returns to a normal schedule.

Mourning Customs: In general, there are no specific mourning customs or anniversary observances. Church denominations that have mourning customs are noted later in this chapter.

Notes: At Evangelical Christian funerals I have attended, the pastor almost always takes the opportunity to remind attendees, whether Christian or not, to seek salvation while they still live. While some will make a gentle reference about coming to Jesus, others might make some members of the audience quite uncomfortable.

Roman Catholic and Orthodox funerals have significant differences from Protestant church services. The presence of a body at the funeral is a key part of the ritual, hence the Church's historical resistance to cremation. The Roman Catholic Church has loosened its restriction on cremation, but still prefers the body be cremated after the funeral.

If you seek the customs of a particular religious tradition that is not included, or for more details on each religion's history, beliefs, and funeral practices, you may wish to consult this excellent resource, *The Perfect Stranger's Guide to Funerals and Grieving Practices: A Guide to Etiquette in Other People's Religious Ceremonies* (SkyLight Paths Publishing, 2000, Woodstock, VT).

An excellent resource for theological insights into major religions is *How Different Religions View Death and Afterlife*, edited by Christopher Jay Johnson, PhD and Marsha G. McGee, PhD (The Charles Press, Publishers, 1998, Philadelphia, PA).

You can also find funeral etiquette information online at www.Funeralwise.com. While I've included many religions here, my apologies if you don't find details on a specific faith tradition you seek.

African Methodist Episcopal (AME) Church

US churches include African Methodist Episcopal, African Methodist Episcopal Zion, African Union First Colored Methodist Protestant Church, Christian Methodist Episcopal Church, and Union American Methodist Episcopal Church. Together they comprise over 5.4 million adherents. Local churches are called "charges." The mourners may receive condolence calls at home after the funeral, and it is appropriate for guests to visit for about thirty to forty-five minutes.

Baptist

There are an estimated 34 million Baptists in the US with dozens of smaller denominations. The two largest Baptist denominations are the Southern Baptist Convention (more than 15 million members) and the National Baptist Convention, USA Inc. (about 8 million members, the largest African-American religious association in the United States).

Cremation is allowed but not encouraged. The family may hold a reception at the church, home, or a restaurant, where food is served, but generally not alcohol. There are no specific Baptist mourning customs or formal remembrance in church, but the family of the deceased may hold their own commemoration at the anniversary of the death.

Buddhist

Buddhists comprise less than one percent of the US population, with perhaps as many as 1.5 million adherents. There are different observances for Tibetan, Japanese, Chinese, Cambodian, Thai, and Ceylonese (now Sri Lankan) Buddhist traditions, but all believe each individual passes through many reincarnations. Buddhists also believe one enters a new incarnation immediately after death, although the resulting being may not be fully realized for nine months.

It's usually not considered appropriate to communicate with the bereaved before the funeral, but it is appropriate to visit the bereaved at home after the funeral. It is appropriate to send flowers to the funeral or make a donation to a charity or cause specified by the family. However, it is not appropriate to send food.

In many cultural traditions, the washing and dressing of the body is a ceremony unto itself. The body is put on display during a wake, with the body preserved by dry ice or embalming. Candles, flowers, burning incense, and other items are placed around the body during viewing.

The Buddha's body was cremated, and this set the example for Buddhists throughout the world to follow. While many choose cremation, some may opt for burial. Guests may attend the interment or cremation.

At cremations, the family may provide a printed pamphlet with Buddhist teachings as a tribute to the deceased and a way of helping their "merit transference," a way for the living to generate good energy toward the deceased for his or her new incarnation. At graveside, prayers are recited and the body is committed to the ground. The local language is used in the ceremony.

In certain Japanese traditions, the funeral takes place within one week. A minister or priest officiates at a ceremony that may last over an hour. Japanese Buddhist funerals can include a ceremony at a funeral home with a eulogy and prayers. In the Japanese tradition, guests are advised to wear dark, somber clothing.

Buddhist traditions from Cambodia, Sri Lanka, and Thailand involve three ceremonies conducted by monks: one, held at the home within two days of death; a second, at the funeral home two to five days after death; and a third, held either at the home or a temple seven days after the burial or cremation. Each ceremony lasts about forty-five minutes. Cambodian, Thai, and Sri Lankan traditions call for attendees to wear white clothing.

All Buddhist traditions and sects quote from the Sutras, the collected sayings of the Buddha. The priest or monk will announce the order of the ceremony. The three components of any Buddhist funeral ceremony are: sharing, the practice of good conduct, and meditation. The body is always viewed in an open casket and guests are expected to view the body, as a valuable reminder of the impermanence of life. When viewing, bow slightly toward the body.

For a funeral ceremony held at a temple or home, seating may be on meditation cushions on the floor. Guests of other faiths should stand when others do so. The vast majority of Buddhist temples allow casual attire for funerals. Loose, comfortable clothing is recommended, especially for temples in which attendees sit on meditation cushions on the floor. Call the temple in advance of the funeral to learn seating details.

It's appropriate to visit the bereaved at home after the funeral. Seven days after burial or cremation, monks in the Cambodian, Thai, and Sri Lankan traditions lead a merit transference ceremony at the home. After the ceremony, food is served.

All Buddhist traditions have a memorial service ninety days after the death. A merit transference ceremony is also held a year after the death, held either at the home of the bereaved or at a temple. When the mourner returns to work and resumes a normal social schedule is up to the individual.

Episcopalian and Anglican

When there's a death in the family, the Episcopal Church expects families to call the priest first before calling the funeral home, and to allow the clergy to direct the funeral. There are approximately 2.5 million Episcopalian/Anglican adherents in the US.

In this Christian denomination, the body is rarely viewed and the casket is kept closed at the funeral. A vigil or wake with a closed coffin may be held at the church or funeral home before the funeral. Cremation after the funeral and the use of embalming are both accepted.

The funeral can be a ceremony in itself or part of a larger service called a requiem, which includes a Holy Communion service. A priest leads the service, which includes the entry rite, opening anthems, announcements, the Liturgy of the Word (Scripture readings), a homily, the Prayers of the People, communion, and a commendation before going to the cemetery or crematorium. There is a variation for a memorial service with cremains or no body present. The *Book of Common Prayer* and a hymnal are used.

At graveside, anthems are sung as the casket is lowered into the grave and the body is committed to the ground with prayers. The priest, family, and friends cast earth upon the casket. A committal rite can also be held at a crematorium or burial at sea.

Guests may visit the bereaved at home after the funeral. Food and alcohol will be served at the family's discretion — ask if it's appropriate to send food. Obituary notices will indicate if flowers are appropriate or if memorial contributions should be made instead.

Greek Orthodox and Other Orthodox Churches

Greek Orthodox funeral traditions have a number of similarities to other Orthodox sects, as well as some significant differences. Other Orthodox Churches include: Antiochian Orthodox, Carpatho-Russian Orthodox, Romanian Orthodox, Russian Orthodox, Serbian Orthodox, and Ukranian Orthodox. The total number of Orthodox adherents in the US is estimated at almost 4.2 million.

Cremation is frowned upon by the Church and can be a cause to deny holding an Orthodox funeral. A wake or viewing may be held at the mortuary the night before the funeral — an appropriate time for eulogies by family or friends, and a priest may hold a Trisagion Service, which includes the singing of hymns and a homily. The body is usually viewed during the funeral.

The Greek Orthodox funeral ceremony is typically held in a church, usually within two to three days of the death (can be up to one week after). The ceremony can last thirty to sixty minutes, and is not part of a larger service. The priest will lead the Trisagion Service, and several books may be used, including *The Divine Liturgy of St. John Chrysostom*. The casket is open throughout the service with a procession passing the casket to pay last respects to the deceased. Greek Orthodox will not schedule a funeral on a Sunday or on Holy Saturday.

In other Orthodox churches, the officiants at a funeral include a bishop and/or priest, and the deacon, subdeacon, and altar server, all of whom assist the bishop or priest. In most Orthodox churches, only officiating bishops and priests use a text at a funeral ceremony.

In the American Carpatho-Russian Church, the Eucharistic liturgy is often celebrated in addition to the funeral service at the discretion of the family, a ceremony of up to ninety minutes.

If there is a Eucharistic liturgy celebrated at a funeral, guests who are not Orthodox do not partake in Holy Communion.

When viewing the body, which is optional but often expected, approach and pause briefly in front of the casket. A Christian might also cross himself or herself and kiss the cross or icon resting on the casket. Greek Orthodox adherents traditionally bow before the casket and kiss an icon or a cross placed on the chest of the deceased.

Traditional Greek Orthodox greetings to the bereaved family are: "May you have an abundant life," "Memory eternal," and "May their memory be eternal." Antiochian Orthodox expressions of sympathy include "May God give you the strength to bear your loss," and "May his [or her] memory be eternal."

At graveside, there is a brief prayer ceremony. The officiating priest or bishop usually puts soil on top of the casket formed in the shape of a cross and each person present places one flower on the casket or spreads the soil. The flowers usually come from those sent to the church for the funeral and then conveyed to the cemetery with the casket.

It is appropriate to briefly visit the bereaved at home after the funeral. Religious objects that a visitor may see there are icons (two-dimensional artistic images of saints), a lighted candle, and burning incense.

A "Meal of Mercy" is provided by members of the family or the deceased's congregation. This reception may be held in the church hall, a restaurant, or the home of the deceased shortly after the burial. Antiochian Orthodox Church funeral receptions usually feature coffee, pastries, and/or fruit.

The bereaved usually stays at home from work for one week. In some cases, widows may avoid social events for a full year. Mourners usually avoid social gatherings for the first forty days after the death and may also wear only black clothing during that time period. Greek Orthodox widows may wear black up to two years. A memorial service is held on the Sunday closest to the fortieth day after the death. A memorial service is then held annually on the anniversary of the death.

Hindu

There are approximately one million Hindus in the United States. Hinduism, the majority religion in India, teaches that although the physical body dies, the individual soul has no beginning and no end. After death, a person's soul is reincarnated into another life form. *Karma*, or the consequences of one's actions, dictates the condition of the deceased's reincarnation.

The body is usually viewed and cremated within twenty-four hours. If the body is cremated within this time frame, embalming is unnecessary. Flowers may be sent to the home to be laid at the feet of the deceased. Donations are not customary, and it is not appropriate to send food. Guests may attend the cremation/funeral ceremony, called *mukhagni*. Men and women should wear white casual clothing to the funeral.

The funeral ceremony takes place at the cremation site. A Hindu priest will lead the ceremony using special books that contain mantras for funeral services, or a senior member of the family may conduct the ceremony. There is usually no program, although the priest may occasionally explain the ceremony to guests who are not Hindus. Portions of the ceremony may be spoken in Sanskrit, the ancestral language of India, as well as the local vernacular. Guests are expected to reverentially view the body but not touch it. A last food offering is made to the deceased and then the body is cremated.

A *shraddha* ceremony is held at home ten days after the death for members of the Brahmin caste and thirty days after the death for members of other castes. This ritual meal is intended to liberate the soul of the deceased from wandering, and brings the family's period of mourning and ritual impurity to a close. It is appropriate to visit the bereaved before the *shraddha* ceremony and attend the service. Visitors are expected to bring fruit.

Mourners dress, eat, and behave austerely during the ten to thirty days after the death and before the *shraddha* ceremony. A mourner may return to a normal work and social schedule after this ceremony. There are rituals for observing the anniversary of the death, which are performed by a priest in a temple.

Islam

There are approximately eight million Muslims in the United States. The Shia and Sunni funeral traditions are similar — variations are dictated by local cultural influences around the world.

Muslim funeral traditions are remarkably similar to Jewish funeral traditions. The body is washed and wrapped in a white cloth shroud. Traditionally, Muslims are never cremated or embalmed and the body is never put on display for viewing, as they believe it violates the dignity of the deceased. Autopsy is prohibited, unless requested by court order.

Ideally, a funeral takes place within twenty-four hours of the death, but in the US it's likely to be scheduled within two to three days. The service will be held at a mosque or funeral home and usually lasts thirty to sixty minutes.

The funeral is a very simple ceremony conducted by an *imam*. Readings from the Qur'an may be used and no program is provided. Arabic is the liturgical language of Islam. Selected prayers and sayings may be in Arabic and the rest of the service conducted in the local vernacular. Guests of other faiths are not expected to do anything other than sit.

Appropriate attire for men is a casual shirt and slacks. For women, a dress that covers the arms and a hem below the knee is recommended, and a scarf is required to cover the head. Dark somber colors are advised. Openly wearing crosses, Stars of David, jewelry with the signs of the zodiac, and pendants with faces or heads of animals or people is discouraged.

Guests should attend the interment. At graveside, the imam leads *janaza* prayers for the dead and the deceased is buried. If the cemetery permits, the body is traditionally buried in a shroud, lying on its right side facing Mecca. It is prohibited to step over, lean on, or sit on a grave.

It is appropriate to visit the home of the bereaved during the forty days of mourning that follow a death. Individuals can set the number of mourning days they actually observe. When visiting, shake hands or hug and kiss only those family members of your same gender, sit and talk quietly with the bereaved and other visitors.

Often, women in the local Muslim community prepare food for mourners and their guests. It is appropriate to send flowers or food, but be aware of the Muslim *halal* food requirements, which includes the avoidance of pork and alcohol.

The mourner usually returns to work after a few days. There is no Islamic prescription on when to return to a normal social schedule, which is more culturally than religiously determined. Women may refrain from normal social activities for forty days after the death of a member of their immediate family, although men might not observe that norm.

The Qur'an dictates a waiting period of four months and ten days (called the *Edda*) for a woman to mourn the death of her husband. During this time, she does not wear bright clothes, use any makeup or perfume, or put on adornments. One cultural norm is for the bereaved to wear black. There are no rituals to observe the anniversary of the death.

Judaism

There are four movements in Judaism with differing levels of ritual observance and attitudes toward the afterlife and treatment of the body. In terms of theology, Reform Judaism is at the most liberal end of the spectrum, followed by Reconstructionist, Conservative, and Orthodox (both traditional and modern). There are approximately 4.1 million Jews in the United States.

The body is ritually washed and dressed in special white cotton or linen clothing, also known as shrouds, by the volunteers of the *Chevra Kaddisha*, local Jewish burial organizations. Embalming is traditionally prohibited, although some funeral homes have reported the use of embalming by secular Jews. The body is never put on display as this is considered disrespectful of the earthly vessel that held the spirit.

Traditional Jewish law forbids cremation, but it is allowed among Reform Jews, who also allow organ donation to help save lives and body donation to further medical knowledge. Autopsy is prohibited, unless requested by court order.

Funerals usually take place the day after the death, ideally within twenty-four hours. However, with modern refrigeration, more liberal Jews will take up to two or three days before burial to allow time for immediate family members to travel from afar. Jewish holidays, the Sabbath (Saturdays), or extraordinary circumstances are acceptable reasons for delay.

At Orthodox, Conservative, Reconstructionist, and some Reform funerals, men will be asked to wear a small head covering, called a *yalmulke* or *kippah*. Women might wear a hat or small veil for a head covering at some Conservative funerals. Women at Orthodox funerals should wear clothing that covers the arms, with dress or skirt hems that fall below the knees, and a head covering, such as a hat or veil.

The funeral service can be held at a synagogue/temple, a funeral home, or graveside. The service usually lasts fifteen to sixty minutes. A rabbi officiates and delivers a eulogy; a cantor sings, leading several prayers and psalms. Some of the prayers and psalms will be spoken in Hebrew and may or may not be translated. The majority of the service is conducted in the local vernacular.

Family members or friends may also deliver eulogies. A program may indicate participants, but not necessarily the order of the ceremony. No books are used.

Family and close friends should attend the interment, which is optional for acquaintances. Graveside services vary depending on the family's background and religious affiliation. At its simplest, the rabbi recites prayers and leads the family in the Mourner's *Kaddish*, a prayer that does not mention death, but reaffirms God's greatness, and *Malei Rachamim*, "Source of Compassion,"a prayer that asks for eternal rest for the deceased.

A traditional service includes a slow procession of the casket to the grave with seven pauses along the way. Seven is the number of completion in the Jewish tradition. Family members put one shovelful of earth into the grave, and guests may also participate in this custom. As the closest family members leave the gravesite, they pass between two rows of relatives and friends.

After the burial, the family sits in mourning at home for seven days, a period of time called *shiva*. Visitors arriving from the cemetery will find a pitcher of water at the door to wash their hands before entering the home, a cleansing ritual. Visitors express condolences, sit quietly, and talk to other callers. Wait to be spoken to by the principal mourners. A "Meal of Condolence" is served at the home after the burial.

Traditionally, a short religious service of ten to twenty minutes is held twice daily in the home, morning and evening. Non-Jews may silently read the English and stand with others during the service. Some Jews might observe *shiva* for just a few days and hold only an evening service at home. Food will most likely be served after the services in the home.

Traditions at the house of mourning include covering mirrors and burning a seven-day memorial candle that is lit after the burial. In a more traditional Jewish home, immediate family members may sit on small chairs or boxes; wear a black ribbon that has been torn or cut and sport slippers or socks rather than shoes. Men will forgo shaving for the week.

A mourner traditionally stays away from work for a week. The mourner may return to a normal social schedule after a month to one year, depending on the deceased's relation to the person, as well as individual inclination. For eleven months, those who follow traditional practice will attend daily morning and/or evening services at the synagogue, to recite the Mourner's *Kaddish* prayer for the deceased.

The anniversary of the death, called a *yahrzeit*, is marked with the lighting of a twenty-four-hour candle at home and attending services in the synagogue, where the deceased's name is read as part of a list with others who died at the same time of year.

The installation of the permanent grave marker usually takes place around the first anniversary of the death. The marker may be installed as soon as *shiva* is completed, or up to eighteen months after the death. Attendance at the simple ceremony of unveiling the headstone is by specific invitation only.

It is not appropriate to send flowers to Jewish mourners. Charitable contributions made in memory of the deceased are customary, and usually indicated in the obituary. Food may be sent to the home of the bereaved, but you may want to check if the family keeps kosher so you can send food that conforms to the Jewish dietary laws.

Lutheran

There are two major Lutheran denominations in the United States: the Evangelical Lutheran Church in America and the Lutheran Church – Missouri Synod. Combined, they have approximately 7.8 million adherents.

A Lutheran funeral is a worship service that may include Holy Communion for all Christian attendees. The service for the burial of the dead consists of three parts: the Service of the Word; the Commendation, a prayer asking God to receive the deceased in mercy; and the Committal, usually performed at the interment site. Books used may include the *Lutheran Book of Worship*, *The Lutheran Hymnal*, or *Lutheran Worship*. Ceremonies or tributes of social or fraternal societies are not allowed within the worship service.

While the casket may be open for a last viewing at the entrance of the church or in a funeral home setting, it is closed prior to and throughout the funeral service. If the body is cremated, the Commendation may be held in the crematory chapel, with the Service of the Word held in the church as a memorial service.

Guests should attend the interment. The casket is carried to the grave, and the pastor leads a brief service with readings and prayers, including the Lord's Prayer. The pastor blesses the earth placed on the casket and blesses those gathered at the graveside.

It is appropriate to visit the home of the bereaved after the funeral. If food is served, wait for the saying of grace before eating. It would be impolite not to eat, unless you have dietary restrictions. There may be alcoholic beverages, depending on the family's custom. You may wish to listen to some of Garrison Keillor's monologues from *A Prairie Home Companion* to experience the full flavor of Lutheran gatherings.

Sending flowers or food is appropriate, unless the family expresses otherwise. A charitable contribution made in memory of the deceased is also appropriate. The family may announce the preferred charity through the obituary or funeral program.

Some Lutheran congregations will mark the first anniversary of a death with prayers in church.

Methodist

There are about twenty-three separate Methodist denominations in the United States, with approximately 8.5 million adherents.

A pastor officiates the funeral service, which may include hymns, a homily, and a eulogy by a close friend or family member. A program will indicate the order of the ceremony. Readings may come from a variety of sources.

Guests should attend interment. The pastor recites prayers at the graveside and the body is committed to the earth. If the body has been cremated before the service, the cremains are buried, or put in a vault, or committed to the sea. Military or fraternal rites may be part of the graveside service.

Mormon (Church of Jesus Christ of Latter-day Saints – LDS)

There are approximately 4.3 million Mormon adherents, or members of the Church of Jesus Christ of Latter-day Saints (LDS), in the United States. Because of the LDS belief in life after death, their funerals are more of a family reunion celebration of life, a happy occasion where memories of the deceased are shared and family bonds are rekindled.

Typically, the body is buried in all-white clothing, signifying purity. If the deceased received blessings in a LDS temple, he or she would be dressed in the clothing worn on that occasion. Embalming and cremation are accepted, although cremation is not encouraged. Whether there is an open casket is the family's choice.

The service may be held in a church, a funeral home, or at the graveside, and usually lasts about sixty to ninety minutes. The officer of the church, typically the bishop of the congregation, conducts the service, and speakers deliver eulogies. A program indicating the order of the ceremony is usually distributed to attendees.

The service includes prayers, hymns, one or more eulogies given by family or friends, and a homily. The speakers will use Scriptures and the congregation may use hymnals.

Guests should attend interment unless it is private, which is rare. The grave is dedicated in a prayer offered by a lay priest, who is usually, but not necessarily, a family member related to the deceased.

After the burial, a meal prepared by the "Relief Society," the women's organization of The Church of Jesus Christ of Latter-day Saints, is served to the family and guests. No alcoholic beverages are served.

Presbyterian

The Presbyterian Church (USA) is the result of at least ten different denominational mergers over the last 250 years. There are approximately 3.6 million adherents in the United States.

The body is rarely viewed, but the family may do so at a visitation event at the funeral home before the funeral. The funeral follows the order for Sunday worship with prayers added for the deceased. A pastor or minister leads the worship service, musicians contribute songs during the service, and family or friends give eulogies.

The service may include psalms, hymns, eulogies, and a homily. The family may request a celebration of the Lord's Supper. The primary books used are a hymnal and a Bible. Any civic or military rites should be conducted separately from a Presbyterian worship service, and can be incorporated at the burial.

Some individuals may not wish to have visitors before or after the funeral, and prefer to mourn in private. Sending flowers and/or food is appropriate. Contributions are not customary, although the family may suggest contributions to charity in lieu of flowers.

Roman Catholic

There are more than 61 million Roman Catholics in the United States, encompassing many different ethnic traditions.

Funerals usually take place within two to three days, possibly up to one week after the death. The first day after a death is usually reserved for the family to make arrangements for the funeral. The second day is often reserved for a wake or visitation, which is commonly held at a funeral home and may possibly last two days. The body is usually viewed at the visitation event, and possibly at the funeral.

The wake provides an opportunity for the community to gather, pray, express their sympathies, and pay their respects. The style of the wake varies depending on the ethnicity of the deceased and his or her family. (See Chapter Four for a detailed description of a traditional Irish wake.)

Regarding cremation, the Catholic Church does allow the celebration of the Funeral Liturgy in the presence of cremated remains, but strongly prefers that the body of the deceased be present for its funeral rites and cremation to take place afterward. The cremated remains are due the same respect as the remains of the body, and the Church dictates that cremains must be buried in a cemetery, entombed in a columbarium, or buried at sea.

Roman Catholic funeral rites include a Vigil Service celebrated in the funeral home or the church the day or evening before the funeral, the Funeral Mass in the church, and the Rite of Committal of the body at the cemetery.

The Vigil Service includes the recitation of the rosary with a priest and eulogies by family or friends. The priest conducts the funeral liturgy, which includes a Mass, and the Rites of Burial. The service includes readings from the Bible, singing of hymns, and Holy Communion. Books include a hymnal, the New American Bible and a prayer book, also called a missal.

Guests of other faiths are expected to stand with the congregation. It is optional for others to kneel, read prayers aloud, and sing. Non-Catholics should not receive communion or say any prayers contradictory to the beliefs of their own faith. At graveside, the priest will lead a brief service and commit the body into the ground.

The family may hold a reception after the funeral at home, a restaurant, or other location. Food is served, and possibly alcohol. It is appropriate to send flowers and/or food to the home before or after the funeral or to the funeral home before the funeral. Charitable contributions are not customary unless the family indicates they are appropriate. A Mass is held annually on the anniversary of the death.

Unitarian Universalist

The Unitarian Universalist end-of-life ritual is called a memorial service, whether the body is present or not. The service usually takes place at a funeral home or in a church within one week, but can be held up to a month after death. No two services are alike. The scheduling of the service is up to the family.

The body is rarely viewed at the memorial service. Sometimes a visitation is held prior to the service at the funeral home or church. Cremation and green burial — with no embalming chemicals and a simple casket that allows remains to return to the earth — are common disposition choices.

A minister delivers a sermon and meditation; a eulogist, chosen by the family, delivers a eulogy of the deceased; and a music director and organist/pianist provide music. The service may also include affirmations, poetry, and a benediction. The hymnal, *Singing the Living Tradition*, may be used. At graveside, the minister leads the recitation of prayers and the body is committed to the ground.

The family may receive visitors at home or in a restaurant after the funeral. Food is served, and possibly alcohol. It is appropriate to send flowers and/or food to the home before the memorial service. Memorial contributions may also be made to a fund or charity designated by the family of the deceased.

Native American/First Nations

The funeral customs of Native Americans, known in Canada as First Nations people, involve the community in activities to honor the deceased and support the family. There are 564 tribes in America, approximately 1.9 million people. Each tribe has their own variation on funeral customs, including use of Native languages, symbols, ceremonial objects, and practice. Native people consider the natural world a sacred place, with religious activities attached to specific places. Many also believe that birth, life, and death are all part of an endless cycle.

In a traditional Native American funeral, the family takes care of their own dead. They make all the arrangements, including transporting the body, and they may utilize green burial techniques. Family members wash and dress the body, and place it in a shroud or wooden casket.

The body may "lie in state" to be honored for two to four days before burial, without embalming. With today's modern technology, the body is preserved prior to burial through refrigeration using dry ice.

Marcia Racehorse-Robles, a Shoshone-Bannock Tribal member who runs Bannock Pride with her husband, David, provides funeral education, as well as oak, cedar, and pine caskets to Native families. They live on the Fort Hall Indian Reservation in Idaho.

According to her, "A lot of home death care is common sense. Most families are caring for an elderly loved one at home, bathing, washing their hair, dressing them, and this is an extension of that, after their death."

Among the Shoshone-Bannock, men set up a tipi for the body to lie in honor for several days, women feed visitors, and children help out. The body is never left alone during this time. During this period, children learn the etiquette of entering the tipi and other traditional ways. Some families dress the deceased in full regalia and jewelry, with moccasins for their trip to the next world.

Spanish conquistadors and missionaries brought Catholicism to the nineteen pueblos of New Mexico in the 1500s. These Native Americans added Catholicism to their traditional ceremonies and beliefs to create an interesting mix of rituals that vary by pueblo. Even with their embrace of

Catholicism, many Pueblo people practice green burial techniques.

Every family and tribe has their own traditional way: prayers, songs, smudging, and items that may be buried with the deceased. A medicine man may perform a ceremony in the tribe's native language. Many tribes restrict what bereaved relatives can eat and/or what kind of activities they can engage in after the death of a loved one. The length of time for mourning varies by tribe.

Military Funerals

US military funerals have their own elements that vary by rank. Basic military funeral honors feature an American flag draped over the casket; an honor detail of two or more uniformed military persons, including one being a member of the veteran's parent service of the armed forces; flag folding and presenting; and the playing of *Taps*.

At graveside, the honor detail conducts a flag-folding ceremony, meticulously folding the flag thirteen times, creating a distinctive triangular shape covered by the blue field with white stars. A representative of the veteran's service branch then presents the folded flag to the veteran's next of kin. The protocol is to kneel in front of the recipient, holding the folded flag waist high with the straight edge facing the recipient, while leaning toward the recipient.

Each of the five military branches uses slightly different wording to present the flag. They are:

Army: "As a representative of the United States Army, it is my high privilege to present you this flag. Let it be a symbol of the grateful appreciation this nation feels for the distinguished service rendered to our country and our flag by your loved one."

Navy: "On behalf of the president of the United States and the chief of naval operations, please accept this flag as a symbol of our appreciation for your loved one's service to this country and a grateful Navy."

Marine Corps: "On behalf of the president of the United States, the commandant of the Marine Corps, and a grateful nation, please accept this flag as a symbol of our appreciation for your loved one's service to country and Corps."

Air Force: "On behalf of the president of the United States, the Department of the Air Force, and a grateful nation, we offer this flag for the faithful and dedicated service of (service member's rank and name)."

Coast Guard: "On behalf of the president of the United States, the commandant of the Coast Guard, and a grateful nation, please accept this flag as a symbol of our appreciation for your loved one's service to country and the Coast Guard."

Some military funerals include a three-volley salute, performed by a rifle party of three, five, or seven members — always an odd number. The tradition of using an odd number in gun salutes is traced to an old naval superstition that even numbers are unlucky.

The rifle party points their muzzles over the casket at graveside, standing a distance away so as not to deafen the attendees. If the funeral is conducted indoors, the rifle party fires their volleys outside upon a signal from a funeral director inside. The guns do not fire bullets, but compressed air cartridges.

The funeral ends with the playing of *Taps*, either by a live bugler or more likely, given the few buglers available these days, an electronic recording. *Taps* is played while the honor detail gives a final salute. Many times, veterans' organizations, such as AMVETS, provide the honor detail for military funeral ceremonies.

At Arlington National Cemetery, full military honors for full colonel officers and above (or corresponding ranks in other armed forces branches) may include a horse-drawn caisson for the casket; a rider-less horse, symbolizing a fallen leader; an escort platoon and military band; and in special circumstances, an aerial flyover of Air Force fighter jets in the "Missing Man" formation.

8

I Got It at Costco

Minimizing funeral and burial costs

"Many people take no care of their money
till they come nearly to the end of it,
and others do just the same with their time."
— *Johann Wolfgang von Goethe (1749–1832)*

Funerals are a huge expense in a family budget and advance planning can help reduce costs. When you find out how expensive end-of-life events can be, it's a big motivator to save where you can. There are many ways to cut costs without looking cheap. Some tips covered here regarding veterans' benefits, pre-need shopping around, purchasing a plot, and cremation are also discussed in Chapter Two, "A Grave Undertaking."

Costco and Other Wholesalers

"I got it at Costco" is one of my favorite phrases, as the wholesale giant is a great source for quality products at low prices. They've been in the business of selling caskets, urns, and other funeral goods through their website, Costco.com, since 2004. Retail giant WalMart got into the act when it added caskets and urns to its website, WalMart.com, in October 2009.

Not only can you get discounted funeral merchandise, but consider the goods needed for a reception: the platters of food, the paper or plastic plates, cups, and utensils, coffee, tea, cases of sodas, etc. Costco is a one-stop shop for just about anything related to holding a party!

Pre-Need Shopping Around: Part Two

As detailed in Chapter Two, shop around for the best prices on funeral services and products *before* someone dies. Once you have a dead body on your hands, you are not in a position, emotionally or time-wise, to shop around. Meet with various local funeral homes to get their prices and a feel for how comfortable you are with the people and their facilities. You will find an amazing variation in costs, personalities, and decor.

Cremation: Part Two

Assuming cremation does not interfere with your religious beliefs, cremation is among the least expensive options for disposition. Cremated remains do not need to be buried, so you can eliminate the cost of buying a burial plot. If you skip embalming, viewing, interment of cremains, and memorial services through the funeral home, a cremation can cost under $1,000.

If you want to hold a funeral before a cremation, some funeral homes will rent caskets that have a removable liner. You may still need to buy some kind of container for the body that goes into the retort. The least expensive of these is the equivalent of a cardboard box. Caskets designed for cremation are made of wood, and the least expensive are soft pine, poplar, or composite wood. There's additional information on new trends in cremation caskets in Chapter Three, "We Can Do That?"

If you plan to keep the remains, you don't need a fancy urn. My friends Jim and Elizabeth keep the cremated remains of their deceased family members in the original square cardboard boxes delivered from the crematorium. They are wrapped in beautiful fabrics tied with fancy ribbons and satin cords. You can display photos of loved ones and meaningful objects related to them next to their remains as a shrine to their memory.

Scattering cremains in water or at a meaningful spot on land doesn't cost anything outside of your transportation to get to that special place. For additional ideas on creative ways with cremated remains, see Chapter Four, "It's My Party and I'll Die If I Want To."

Donating the Body: Part Two

Giving your body to science for research costs nothing, but it does require some advance arrangements. You contact a local medical school, sign consent forms, place copies with your advance directives and wills, and arrange for the medical school to be notified when you die.

Cadavers are used for a range of purposes to advance medical knowledge. They can be used for disease research and treatment, surgical education of medical students, medical instrumentation creation and improvement, and tissue and organ studies. One must decide if organs and tissue or the whole body will be donated, as those are two separate programs and procedures.

Most medical schools only accept whole bodies, with the exception of corneal donations, which don't affect the rest of the body. Corneas, the clear surface at the front of the eye, help save eyesight through corneal transplants. They can be harvested at a funeral home, and the procedure will not affect the look of the body if there's to be a viewing. Most eye bank organizations indicate that cornea donors can be of any age, and even people with poor eyesight or cataracts can donate. However, there may be an upper age limit, so check with your local organization.

Physical condition of the body, not age, is the important factor in whole body donation. Most people are eligible for making donations, with the exception of those with communicable diseases, such as hepatitis, HIV/AIDS, and tuberculosis, severe obesity or edema (fluid swelling), or cadavers with decomposition or trauma.

Start the registration process by contacting the medical school to which you wish to donate. Bear in mind, not all schools may have room for cadaver donations at the time of death, so do your research early to find where your body would be most appreciated.

As an alternative, BioGift (www.biogift.org) and MedCure (www.medcure.org) are two medical research and education programs that facilitate full body donations to science at no cost to the family. Beware of fraudulent providers — look for organizations affiliated with the American Association of Tissue Banks (www.aatb.org).

If the family wishes to get the cremated remains sent back, it may take up to two years, depending on how the body is used.

Pre-Purchase a Burial Plot and Casket

If you plan to live out your days in the same town and want to be buried in a local cemetery, investing in a burial plot before you need it can result in savings. After all, real estate prices usually go up, not down, and your final resting place is no exception.

Many cemeteries will offer a financing plan, which adds to the overall cost, but avoids one big out-of-pocket expense. All the cemeteries I'm familiar with require full payment for the plot when you purchase at need (that means, when you have a body you want to bury *now*).

Depending on the type of casket desired, you can realize tremendous savings by purchasing ahead of need from an outside provider. A plain pine box made by a local woodworker can be half the cost of a similar casket provided by a funeral home. The challenge, of course, is where do you keep a casket before you need to use it?

There are woodworkers who make caskets that double as bookcases, coffee tables, wine racks, and entertainment centers, designed to have the shelves removed when the time comes to take out the other stuff and put in a body. There are also coffin kits that fit in a slender cardboard box that can be stored in the garage or under a piece of furniture.

However, keeping a casket at home is considered bad *feng shui*, if you believe in that sort of thing, and you certainly wouldn't want to keep one under your bed. One option is to use a storage locker to keep a pre-need casket offsite, but only if you're already storing other things there. You could easily pay more than the cost of the casket in storage fees.

Military and Veterans Benefits

Those who have served in the military and their spouses and minor age children are entitled to free gravesites and burials in national cemeteries. Veterans' death benefits include a cemetery plot, opening and closing of the grave, and a memorial stone. The federal government will provide a free veteran's memorial stone for placement in other cemeteries, but you have to accept the established format and size for military markers.

Most states have a department of veterans' affairs that can help families obtain services. Other details on military funerals are in

Chapter Two, "A Grave Undertaking," and Chapter Seven, "Amazing Grace."

Members of the military and their dependents can also request whole body burial at sea, done at no cost to the family. However, because the committal ceremony is performed from a United States Navy vessel while the ship is deployed, family members cannot be present.

Direct Burials and Cremations

Undertakers who specialize in direct burials and cremations can cost much less than traditional funeral homes. They provide similar services in less fancy settings than their higher cost competitors, but they get the job done. I've seen one business post their price for a simple cremation on a billboard on a busy street.

Direct burials or cremations give the family the option to bypass a ceremony altogether. However, please consider doing some sort of ritual to acknowledge the death. Those who have lost a loved one can really benefit from the support of their community — that's what funeral rituals are all about.

The Funeral Consumers Alliance and Memorial Societies

Memorial societies are nonprofit educational organizations first started in the late 1930s, in the midst of the Great Depression. This was a time when funerals were becoming increasingly expensive due to the growing use of embalming and elaborately manufactured caskets.

These organizations, most now affiliated with the Funeral Consumers Alliance (FCA), are dedicated to protecting a consumer's right to choose a meaningful, dignified, affordable funeral. They were instrumental in the growth of cremation as a disposal option.

The Funeral Consumers Alliance helps increase public awareness of funeral options, including how to care for your own dead without using a funeral home. They offer advice, consumer news, FAQs, information on legal rights, and provide contacts for local FCA branches on their website: www.Funerals.org.

Federal Trade Commission Information for Consumers

The American Way of Death by Jessica Mitford directed a bright spotlight on US funeral practices in 1963, illuminating how some mortuaries maximized profits and maneuvered the bereaved into buying an expensive funeral. Her exposé helped change federal law, which became The Funeral Rule. The Federal Trade Commission (FTC) provides information about consumer rights under The Funeral Rule. It states:

- You have the right to choose only those goods and services you want (with some exceptions) and to pay only for those you select (you don't have to use "packages" of goods and services that may include items you do not want).
- The funeral provider must state this right in writing on the general price list.
- If state or local law requires you to buy any particular item, the funeral provider must disclose it on the price list, with a reference to the specific law.
- The funeral provider may not charge a fee or refuse to handle a casket you bought elsewhere.
- A funeral provider that offers cremations must make alternative cremation containers available.

The FTC offers *Funerals: A Consumer Guide*, as well as brochures and other detailed information to help consumers make their best choices when planning for a funeral. The FTC's website for information regarding The Funeral Rule is www.ftc. gov/bcp/edu/microsites/funerals/coninfo.htm.

Online Suppliers of Funeral Goods

There's a mind-boggling array of low-cost funeral suppliers on the Internet, other than Costco.com. There are sites featuring discounted goods and services you didn't know you needed: funeral programs, prayer cards, crucifixes, keepsake items, eco-friendly burial, pet memorialization, roadside memorial markers, etc. As always, comparison shop before you buy, and don't always assume something you find online will be cheaper than something you can buy locally.

Reducing Reception Costs

The costs for a reception following the funeral or memorial service can add up, depending on what the family chooses to do. Going to a restaurant makes it easy, paying others to do the serving and cleaning up, but then there is the bill to pay at the end.

Holding a gathering at home, you can serve food that has been thoughtfully provided by concerned friends and neighbors. You may have a lot of cleaning up on your hands, but your friends may offer to help with that, as well.

You can request of those who ask what they can do to help to provide specific food or drink for the reception. For example, at one memorial service I coordinated, we held a reception in the social hall of the church. We asked attendees to bring cookies, and they provided an amazing, generous array.

The out-of-pocket expense for the reception was minimal, yet the tea and cookies served were lovely. While the refreshments were consumed, there was ample time for all to speak about the deceased and comfort the bereaved.

Remember, you can still cut costs, have a meaningful, memorable event, and not look cheap!

9

Where's Fido?

What to do when a pet dies

*"Animals are such agreeable friends—
they ask no questions, they pass no criticisms."*
— *George Eliot (1819–1880),*
"Mr. Gilfil's Love Story,"
Scenes of Clerical Life, 1857

Anyone who loves and loses a pet knows the intense pain we feel when an animal companion dies. These are beings that give us unconditional love and look to us for their well-being. How we treat our pets, as well as the people we love, reflects our core values.

It's rare that headline news strikes our families directly, but the big news in 2007 about tainted pet food from China hit my family hard.

My brother Glen had to put down his twelve-year-old Great Dane, Abby, because her kidneys were failing and she couldn't hold her bladder. He had switched three months earlier from feeding her Alpo to Iams Canned Chicken & Chunks, one of the recalled foods, thinking at the time it would be better for her digestion. It may be that both brands were tainted.

He cried for three days before she was euthanized. The vet took care of disposing the body. "I don't think you get as much closure when you put them down and you don't have the body to dispose of," Glen said.

I know about feeling guilty over the death of a dog. Many years ago, I let our family's basset hound, Lady, out one cold winter day. I didn't walk her because I was sick in bed. A neighbor called to say a car on a busy road around the corner from our house had hit Lady.

My penance was burying her body. I'm sure it was totally against local ordinances in Maryland. I transported her stiff remains, wrapped in an old comforter, by wheelbarrow to the back edge of our property. Digging dirt in freezing, nasty East Coast weather was hard work.

Still, the physical effort was a release for the emotional burden. With tears, sweat, and a runny nose, I buried her and placed a large rock to mark the spot. It was a comfort to see her resting place in the backyard, and seeing any basset hound still delights me. And Glen got another dog within a year of Abby's death — a tri-colored basset hound with a big personality named Charlie.

For my parents' twenty-fifth wedding anniversary, my brothers and I gave them a small parrot — actually, a white-eyed conure. We thought Condo was a fun gift.

That bird lived almost thirty years, during which my mother changed the paper in its cage, saved the seeds from peppers and cantaloupe as bird treats, and swept up the mess it constantly made. It laughed the same way the family did, chuckling along whenever something funny was said. We never did find out if it was male or female, but it usually tried to bite men and cooed at women.

After it died, my parents put Condo in a sock shroud and buried it in the front yard of their Florida home, right next to a Bird of Paradise plant — an appropriate spot for a bird that has gone to its final roost.

A week after the bird died, I asked my parents how they were doing. Dad missed saving the papers to line the cage, and Mom thought of Condo every time she cut up a pepper. They both missed the cheery "Hello" the bird called every time they walked in the house. It took some time to get over the loss after thirty years of company.

Euthanasia and Pet End-of-Life Issues

We humans agonize over choices we must make when a pet is sick, injured, in pain, or suffering from deterioration due to advanced age. An ailing pet never ceases to be family. As humans, we have the power to relieve their pain with humane euthanasia.

A couple I know, Mark and Merri, made the painful choice to euthanize their suffering dog, Lucky, after they recognized that no amount of medical intervention was going to improve his quality of life. The veterinarian came to their home, and in the backyard that he played in, administered the shots. He passed peacefully, cradled in their arms.

Mark explained their approach: "Merri and I started talking about euthanasia for Lucky months before it became inevitable. I'm glad we did. Though nothing makes the decision easy, I think it helped us both that we didn't have to decide under any extra pressure."

"Even in the two months prior to Lucky's death, we switched back and forth as to which of us was more ready to accept it," he said. "For a long time, I thought if Lucky had any good moments, they made life worth living. Eventually, I realized that five good minutes with a bone might not offset five hours pacing in pain. Not that it ever became a calculation, but it was an effort to gauge his quality of life."

Mark continued, "I would stress how important and helpful it was to us to have him euthanized at home. We've had three cats euthanized at the vets. Although those euthanasia experiences were humane and compassionate, being at home and not adding the stress to Lucky or us of getting to the vet made a huge difference."

"The hardest phone call I ever made involved scheduling his death. I sobbed on the floor next to him after that. Having his long-time vet perform the euthanasia also helped us all. Turning the spot he last lived into a garden gives us an ongoing memorial to a great friend and loved one."

The good news for ailing Fido and Fluffy is that pet hospices are becoming more prevalent across the country. The same type of supportive end-of-life care that humans can receive, including pain relief and emotional support for the family, are available for dogs, cats, and other animals.

Our animal companions cannot speak in words, but we can hear their pain. As caretakers of our pets, we are in the difficult position of choosing when and how to relieve their pain. Some will opt to take a medical intervention route in the hope of postponing their grief over the animal's death, relieving guilt by being able to say, "We did all that we can," and spending a lot of money in the process.

Some will opt for humane euthanasia, surrendering to the inevitable that comes to all, whether animal or human. Yes, it avoids huge veterinary bills, but it also prevents a beloved pet from further suffering. It may be a better choice to lovingly put a pet to sleep, in the comfort of the family home, rather than subject it to more medical intervention that may not help.

Estate Planning for Pets

My friend Barbara has six cats and no spouse or kids. After a brush with heart problems, she prepared her will and set up a pet trust for her kitties. When she dies, her cats will be cared for and live out their days in her house, which will become property of a local animal rescue organization.

A pet trust provides a legal technique to make sure beloved animal companions are cared for after the human is gone. You basically give your pet to a trusted person — a trustee — along with enough money or other property for them to make arrangements for the proper care of your pet. The trustee then pays a monthly stipend to the named caretaker(s) for your pet. The caretaker actually feeds the animal, plays with it, takes it for walks and to the vet, etc.

"You want to make sure the caretaker is willing to take on the responsibility of caring for your cat or dog and that they are in a position to handle it," said Steve Hartnett of the American Academy of Estate Planning Attorneys.

You should name up to three alternate caretakers, in case your first choice is unable or unwilling to serve. To avoid having your pet end up without a home, consider naming a sanctuary or no-kill shelter as your last choice.

There are two types of pet trusts: a "living" trust that is in effect while you are still alive, or a "testamentary" trust that takes effect after you die through provisions in your will. A living trust avoids a delay in property being available for the pet's care after a death or disablement, but they often have additional start-up costs and administration fees.

A testamentary trust is a less expensive option, but there may not be funds available to care for the pet between when you die and when your will is probated. Also, it does not apply to a disability that may make you unable to care for your pet.

With either pet trust type, you'll need to transfer money or other property into the trust, known as funding. Without funding, the trustee will not be able to provide your pet with care. There are many factors in deciding how much money to transfer into the pet trust, including the type of animal, its life expectancy, the standard of living you wish to provide, potentially expensive medical treatment, and the overall size of your estate.

To get a pet trust, consult with an attorney who specializes in estate planning, and if possible, also has experience with pet trusts. While you're at it, do some estate planning for your human family, as well!

What to Do with Pet Remains

"If you want to highly insult a dog owner, don't ever say 'It was just a dog'," said dog lover Yvonne Blevins. "For most true pet owners, it is very devastating when they lose them." Can you imagine someone saying, "It was just a person," to a bereaved family member?

Yvonne and her husband, Roger, have the cremated remains of four deceased pets in their own memorial rose garden in the back yard of their home. The childless couple considers their dogs as family. They have sandstone monuments etched with the name of each pet, their nickname, years of life, and a picture.

The Blevins did their own personal memorial services for their dogs, different for the personality of each animal. If they ever move, they will take the cremains, which are in boxes wrapped in plastic, and the headstones to their new home.

Pet owners can process their grief in many different ways, starting with the disposal of the body. What you do with your pet's remains can vary widely, depending on where you live, how you feel about the remains, how other members of your family feel about "what to do with Fido," your budget, and other factors. Here are some options to consider:

1. Let the vet handle it. If an animal companion dies while at the vet's or is euthanized in the vet's office, they will offer to dispose of the body. In the midst of grief, this is an easy way to deal with your pet's remains, although perhaps not the most healing. You may not have a say in how the body is disposed of, and you may miss a sense of closure. This service may or may not have an associated cost.

2. Get the remains cremated. Options for cremated remains abound. You can keep Fluffy in a special container and create an altar to her memory with her photo and cat toys. This is a viable avenue if you rent or live in an apartment or condo. You can scatter the ashes in your yard or a special spot where your pet liked to play. You can bury ashes in your backyard and place a memorial marker.

Pet cremation costs vary based on the size of the animal, and how the cremation is handled. For example, Best Friends Pet Services in Albuquerque offers two individual cremation options: one, where the pet is by itself during the cremation; the other, where it is separated from other pets in the retort, using ceramic dividers. The remains are returned in a ceramic urn. With the third option, communal cremation, a group of pets is cremated and the remains are not returned, but scattered on private land.

3. Bury the body in your yard. This gets a little trickier. Cities and municipalities have a wide range of zoning ordinances regarding burial of animal and human remains. You can check with your local land planning and zoning office to find out the rules for your area. In rural areas where folks own lots of land, this isn't as much of a concern.

Either way, remember to dig deep enough so the remains are not disturbed or become a health hazard. Check with all family members first to see if they are okay with having a "body" in the yard. All it costs is your own muscle, sweat, and tears. You can pay for a memorial stone if you wish.

4. Bury the body in a pet cemetery. While a formal cemetery burial for a pet can be an expensive option, they can be some of the sweetest resting places for a beloved animal. You get a sense of the love that others lavished on their deceased pets, and it's comforting to be among other pet lovers when you visit your pet's grave. Prices for services and perpetual care can vary widely.

You can find an online listing of pet cemeteries and crematoria at the website for the International Association of Pet Cemeteries and Crematories, www.IAOPC.com.

5. Check with your local humane society. If you don't have a place to bury a pet or the funds for disposal fees, your local humane society may be able to receive and dispose of animal remains for little or no charge.

Holding a Pet Funeral

Should you do a funeral or memorial service for your pet? Some kind of ceremony that recognizes the loss is a valuable undertaking, especially when children are involved.

However, you may want to keep it a small immediate family affair, with those who were closest to the pet. Some people don't hold pet death in the same regard as the end of a human life. They can brush aside your feelings with "It was just a dog," and do you serious emotional harm.

Many of the elements that provide comfort in a human funeral apply to a pet funeral.

Recognize Reality: Acknowledge that the pet has died, talk about how it came into the family, lived a good life, and was loved by those gathered around.

Remember: Share stories about the pet's antics or personality traits, actions undertaken on the pet's behalf, and treasured memories. You might gather photos, toys, and other memorabilia related to the pet.

Reaffirm Beliefs: If you believe your pet has gone to a better place, say so. If you believe you will be reunited with your pet when you leave this world, say so. If you believe the love of an animal companion is a valuable thing, say so.

Release: Close by gently saying goodbye. Cover the grave with earth and set any memorial marker or tributes in place.

Our beloved pets' spirits live on in our hearts forever.

Grieving Pet Loss

Santa Fe grief counselor Janice Barsky decided there was a need for a pet loss support group when a woman who had been hospitalized from traumatic grief over the death of her dog showed up at a hospice grief support group meeting she was facilitating.

The group was outraged at the woman's attendance, along the lines of "How dare you sit there and talk about the loss of your pooch, when I lost my husband of fifty years," said Barsky. The woman never returned.

When people don't get support from society for their loss, they experience what's called disenfranchised grief. Those who are uncomfortable talking about death, don't know what to say, or are truly careless, may casually dismiss the loss if a pet. Yet, the pain is very real, sometimes debilitating, and requires time to heal.

"Nothing is quite so devastating as losing a pet," said Jon Marr, owner of Braemarr's Loving Care Pet Cemetery and Crematory. "They love us so utterly, unconditionally, and without judgment under every and all circumstances; it's small wonder our pets often become our closest companions as we travel this road of life."

"There's just something special about a person who's willing to emotionally invest in a creature, let them so deep into their heart and form that strong bond, knowing, at some level, in all likelihood, they're going to outlive them," said Barsky.

With that deep love, comes deep loss when the animal dies, and pet owners find different ways to cope.

Marilyn Saltzman, former general manager of Best Friends Pet Services in Albuquerque, which provides cremation, memorialization, and tributes for pets, saw different emotional reactions for the loss of human versus animal family members.

When a pet dies, it is a highly emotional time, and gradually the grief diminishes. With a human death, the family is often in shock as they make funeral arrangements, and then grief intensifies as the days go by.

"The key to remember is grief is normal and you'll move through it. It feels sometimes like you won't, but you will," said Ann Beyke, an Albuquerque counselor who specializes in pet loss grief. Common emotions, besides profound sadness, include anger, guilt, and depression.

Beyond losing the love of the animal, the pet represents cycles of life. Duffy Swan, president of French Funerals and Cremations, which owns Best Friends Pet Services, spoke of a kitten that was a present to his daughter for her fourth birthday.

The cat moved with the family to several cities and was always there as the daughter grew up and then got married. He thought the son-in-law would take the cat with his daughter, but no, the cat, which lived to the age of nineteen, stayed with

Swan and his wife. When the cat was ailing, Swan held it as it was euthanized.

"I wasn't that close to the cat, but after I left the vet's, I had this sense of being blue," Swan said. "I later realized that cat was the last living link to my four-year-old daughter, and it was the end of an era."

Counselors Barsky and Beyke agree that talking about the loss with sympathetic people helps to heal the grief.

"I can always tell when a person is getting better in any kind of grief because they start wanting to help others," said Barsky. "That they even notice someone else's distress is a sign of great progress."

Observed Beyke, "Just knowing that others have felt the same thing, are grieving the same way, having the same questions, and getting the support of others is essential during a time like this."

Here are some tips they offer on grieving the loss of a pet:

- Allow yourself to mourn. Tears are natural. Don't apologize for feeling the way you do.
- Do what feels right for you. Don't be afraid to insist on what you need from the vet before a pet is euthanized, such as holding and talking to the animal.
- Change your routine. If you have always taken a walk with your dog at 6:00 A.M., schedule a different activity at that time.
- Seek supportive people. Avoid those who don't understand or say hurtful things.
- Take care of yourself. Grief goes to a physical level quickly. Avoid making yourself sick.
- Push the envelope toward healing. If it's too painful to look at photos of a deceased pet, put it off, but go back again later. It will get easier.

- Don't beat yourself up or replay guilt tapes. "If only..." thoughts drain your emotional energy and interfere with the healing process.
- Wait six months before getting another animal. It's not a set rule, but if you get a replacement pet right away, you might not bond well with the new one.
- Get professional help if you need it. One online resource is the Association for Pet Loss and Bereavement (www.aplb.org).

Memorial Options for Pets

Many service providers have developed to address a need for memorializing deceased pets. You can find more products and services to honor your deceased pet than you thought possible by searching online for "pet memorials."

There are memorial stones and markers for pet graves, garden statuary, urns of ceramic, stone, wood, cloisonné, metal, and other materials for display. You can get beautiful biodegradable urns of paper, fabric, hemp, or wood for burial in earth or water. You can get paw or nose imprints of your pet, and turn them into plaques or jewelry. Turn bits of your pet's cremated remains into gemstones, or obtain clips of fur or feathers. Special picture frames can enshrine your pet's memory. You can even make bookmarks with your pet's image.

And now there are memorial parks that allow humans to be buried with their pets. Sunset Memorial Park in Albuquerque has a unique Best Friends Forever section that is a cremation-only area with wall niches and ground plots for people to spend eternity with their pets.

However you choose to pay tribute to your pet, remember that it's not what you buy, but the feeling that you hold in your heart that truly matters.

10

"What-If" Questions

Pondering out-of-the ordinary situations

"A discovery is said to be an accident meeting a prepared mind."
— *Albert Szent-Gyorgyi, biochemist (1893–1986)*

Many out-of-the-ordinary situations can arise when someone dies. Let's examine a few and how they can be addressed.

What if a person dies one place but needs to go someplace else in the US for burial?

If Aunt Martha dies in Arizona but has a burial plot back east in Massachusetts, what do you do to get her there? You can't just fly Aunt Martha home in the backseat of your Cessna. Driving her there in the back of a pick-up truck is another story.

Shipping a body domestically, while simpler than international shipping, still has many parts to address. International shipping of bodies adds a whole other layer of time and activity to the process. Both domestic and international shipping can be either a quick or lengthy process.

This information comes courtesy of Bill Piet, a funeral director with Porter Loring Mortuaries of San Antonio, Texas, which ships sixty to eighty bodies a year.

Domestic Air Shipment

Whole body shipment by air is handled as airfreight. You need to work with a funeral home to ship a body, as they know what to do, how to handle the paperwork, and provide the proper containers. And in today's post-9/11 world, it's a requirement.

The Transportation Security Administration (TSA) has a "known shipper" policy, which became effective July 1, 2009. It states that all shipments of human remains that originate in the US or its territories must be tendered by a known shipper, which in this case is the funeral home. Funeral homes are required to register with each airline and become part of the TSA Known Shipper database.

If pre-need arrangements have been made with a funeral home at the destination, start the process by contacting them first. The funeral director will then work with a local provider at the origination point. If no arrangements have been done in advance, it's time to get on the phone and do some research for mortuaries at the destination city.

A burial-transit permit is required when transporting a body out of state and for transporting by common carrier (airlines or trains). Permits are obtained from the local health department or county clerk's office (this varies by state) by providing a death certificate.

While a fully completed death certificate can take two or three weeks to obtain, the certificate for a burial-transit permit can be completed by the funeral home with biographical information about the deceased, minus cause of death confirmation. There can be delays getting a permit over weekends and holidays.

Shipping Containers

Within the US, very few states require embalming before shipping, and those states have exceptions for religions, most notably Judaism and Islam, which prohibit embalming. If the body is to be embalmed, it should occur before shipping.

Embalming, or not, impacts the choice of containers for air shipping. An un-embalmed body can be preserved with cool packs in the container. The use of dry ice as a refrigerant in air shipping is now prohibited, as it can pose a danger at high altitudes.

An embalmed body can be shipped in a casket enclosed by a shipping case called an Air Tray, a heavy cardboard box with a wood bottom designed to protect the casket. There's also a combination container specifically designed for body shipment. If the body is not embalmed, the funeral home must use a Ziegler container, a metal box that seals tightly to prevent seepage of fluids or escape of odors. Whatever the container, the burial-transit permit is enclosed in a sturdy envelope and attached to the shipping case.

The cost for these containers varies. One funeral home charges $175 for an Air Tray, $195 for a combination container, and $785 for a Ziegler container. Ziegler containers are typically destroyed after one use.

Air Cargo Considerations

Some considerations when shipping by air include the size of the destination airport — a small airport may only accommodate smaller planes, which don't have large enough cargo space to carry human remains. The smallest plane that can easily carry human remains is an MD80. Most airlines elect not to ship bodies on the popular 737. And most airlines have a carrying limit of 500 pounds gross weight, which includes the body, the casket or container, and the Air Tray — something to keep in mind if the deceased was obese.

The funeral home needs to know the operating hours for an airport's air cargo center, and when to arrive and receive air cargo. It would be a shame if Aunt Martha got parked in air cargo over the weekend when the office is closed.

Another consideration is whether the routing of your precious cargo has airline hub changes. Two hours between flights should be enough time to make sure Aunt Martha makes her connection and gets to her funeral on time.

Taking the Slow Train

Shipping by train, another common carrier, is not done as much as it used to be, but it's still doable and the same regulations as air cargo apply. It can be a most appropriate way to send a loved one home. Bill Piet related how Porter Loring Mortuaries used Amtrak to ship a retired conductor from Texas to St. Louis, Missouri, fulfilling the man's wish to be transported to his final resting place by train.

Driving Miss Daisy

If the destination is drivable, either the funeral home or the family can transport the body by vehicle. In Texas, for a body transported by a funeral director in a company van or SUV, no container is needed.

They can use a cot or stretcher. If *you* are taking Aunt Martha in the family pick-up or minivan, her body must be encased in a container that insures against seepage of fluids or escape of offensive odors, i.e., a sealed casket or Ziegler container. State regulations can vary, so if you're going to do the driving, especially across several states, find out what you need to do from a local funeral home or your state's department of health.

And, if the trip is long, so long that you'll need a good night's sleep along the way, your local funeral director may be able to help arrange for a mortuary in the city where you plan to stop to hold the body in their facilities overnight. We've all heard about items stolen out of vehicles parked at motels.

While I doubt someone would want to steal Aunt Martha's body, it's better to play it safe. And it's more respectful of the body to put it in a secure spot overnight, rather than leaving it out in the parking lot.

Out-of-state transportation requires a burial-transit permit with the body. In-state transportation (in Texas) requires you have a report of death form with the body, but again, check for your particular state's regulations. After all, you wouldn't want to be pulled over by the cops with a dead body in your car and not be able to prove it's really okay.

What if someone dies abroad and the family wants to bring the body back to the US for burial?

Approximately 6,000 Americans die outside of the country every year whose bodies are brought back to the United States. This is in addition to military deaths, which Uncle Sam handles.

"Don't expect this to be a fast process," said funeral director Bill Piet. With every death abroad that is not taken care of by the US military, returning a body is a lengthy process that can take weeks, with numerous long-distance phone calls — many of those calls being international.

Consular Contacts

Start the process by contacting the US embassy or consular office in the country in which the person died. In a foreign country with a different local language, it's easier to communicate with US folks who speak English. A listing of the websites for US embassies, consulates, and diplomatic missions is available at www.USembassy.gov.

If you have difficulty contacting a local embassy, the Department of State's Office of American Citizens Services and Crisis Management in Washington DC is available to assist: (202) 647-5225, online: travel.state.gov/travel/about/who/who _1245.html.

In addition, Overseas Citizens Services, at (202) 501-4444, provides assistance in all matters relating to the death of a US citizen abroad, with twenty-four-hour emergency service.

When an American dies abroad, the consular officer notifies the next of kin or legal representative. A consular services representative assists the family in making arrangements with local authorities for preparation and disposition, following the family's instructions but also in accordance with local laws.

Bear in mind that the family is responsible for all local charges incurred — the US embassy or consulate provides no funding for returning bodies or cremated remains to the United States.

With a death abroad, you need to act quickly and contact the consular office immediately. Some countries require burial after three days, or even sooner, and it can happen without the consent of the family. Many countries require that the body stays buried for two years, and some will not allow disinterment for as long as fifteen years.

Foreign Funeral Homes

Selecting a funeral home abroad is a big challenge. The US government has no agencies or authority to regulate funeral homes in a foreign country. You might shop for a funeral home abroad by checking with a reputable association such as the National Funeral Directors Association or Selected Independent Funeral Homes.

Select the least expensive services available, as charges will have to be paid when services are rendered. Charges stated by the funeral home that will initiate shipping, even if they seem excessive, will have to be paid before the body is shipped. If the family is unable to pay the cost of shipping, which can be many thousands of dollars, cremation or local burial in that foreign country are options.

While you may be tempted to involve US officials, such as senators and congressmen, do **not** try to have them intervene on your behalf. Foreign countries often do not respond well to such pressure and it can actually slow the process down.

Embalming the body for transportation to the US is recommended, given the length of time it takes to make long-distance arrangements and the type of shipping containers available in the country the body will be shipped from (see domestic shipping question). However, embalming is not uniformly available in many countries and it may not be the same process that's done in the United States.

If the family wants to see the body once it has arrived stateside, use caution. Once the remains are under the care of the family's local mortuary, allow the funeral director to determine the condition of the body and perhaps do some cosmetic work before having a viewing.

Paperwork to Process

Shipping a body into the US also requires significant paperwork. The consular services representative in the originating country will assist with the preparation of all documents. These include the consular report of death of an American citizen abroad, certified copies of which will serve as the death certificate; a consular mortuary certificate, used for US customs clearance; an affidavit from the foreign funeral director for US customs, providing evidence of embalming; and a transit permit authorizing export of remains from the country.

And then there are requirements for US entry. If the remains are embalmed and hermetically sealed in a casket that will not be opened prior to burial, the documentation that accompanies the consular mortuary certificate will satisfy US public health requirements.

If the body comes into the country through the Port of New York City, there are additional requirements. The shipment must have a transit or removal permit issued by the country originating the shipment and showing the specific destination: cemetery, city, state.

In addition, airlines cannot transfer to another airline, i.e., from an international line to a domestic one, without securing the services of a New York City funeral director, either going out of or coming into the US. This requirement comes courtesy of the local union of funeral directors.

At this point, you might ask yourself if it wouldn't be easier to have the body cremated and the ashes returned to the United States. See the TSA information about cremated remains on airlines in Chapter Four, "It's My Party and I'll Die If I Want To."

What if someone dies in the US and the family wants to ship the body to another country for burial?

Many of the same considerations for shipping a body into the US from a foreign country apply to shipping a body out of the US. It will be a lengthy process, maybe ten to fourteen days or longer. It will entail numerous long-distance telephone calls. It requires working with embassies or consular offices, although in this case, you would contact the offices for the country that the body will be shipped to.

In addition to phone calls to the consular office, you may be required to visit in person to process paperwork. If you do not live in a major city, you may have to travel quite a distance to reach the nearest consular office for the country to which you will ship the body. They may want to inspect the shipping container, and they may require you use the services of another funeral director.

Each country has their own requirements for the type of shipping container and/or casket that will contain the body. And airline schedules are yet one more consideration that plays a role in how long it takes to accomplish international shipping from the US.

Most funeral homes have two resources at their disposal to locate and contact consulates: The Funeral Home and Cemetery Directory, and The Redbook: The National Directory of Morticians. In addition, the US Department of State offers listings and contact information for embassies and foreign consular offices in the US through this website: www.state.gov/s/cpr/rls/.

If you are trying to send a body to Cuba, North Korea, or Iran, the US has no diplomatic relations with those countries. This will make shipping a body to any of these countries an even longer process.

The receiving country may have requirements regarding embalming or other preparation of the remains for shipping. The bodies headed for burial in the Middle East, mostly unembalmed Jews and Muslims, are sent in the tightly sealed Ziegler metal container. Once the body arrives, however, it's taken out of the metal case and buried in either a shroud or soft wood casket. Often one sees discarded Ziegler cases along roads to cemeteries in Middle Eastern countries, a remnant and reminder of the body's trip home.

What if your family doesn't want to carry out your funeral plans?

If you want something really special or different for your send-off but aren't sure your heirs will carry out your wishes, there are several ways to ensure your funeral plans are executed.

For example, at one talk I gave, an elderly Jewish woman said she wanted cremation but was concerned her more-observant family would not honor her wishes. Or perhaps you want a Viking funeral, where the body is put on a wooden boat that is set ablaze out at sea. How can you make sure your wishes will be honored?

There are three main ways, according to Steve Hartnett, Associate Director of Education for the American Academy of Estate Planning Attorneys.

First, you can put your wishes in your will and name the executor responsible for carrying out those wishes. The drawback: the will may not be read until after the funeral. Unless the executor knows about those particular funeral wishes and participates in the funeral planning, your special send-off may not happen.

Second, you can prepay a funeral plan. Hartnett suggests funding a funeral trust — essentially a paid-up insurance policy that covers the cost of the arrangements. The trust can be designated to pay a funeral home, but it does not lock in specific arrangements.

There is also the option of preplanning and prepaying with a reputable funeral home for specific arrangements, locking in costs and services. Let the family know that these arrangements have already been made and paid for.

Third, you can disinherit anyone who objects to your plans, and let your inheritors know this before you die. This strategy is known as an *in terrorem* (Latin for "to instill terror") or no-contest clause in the will. However, this strategy may not be valid in all states.

Whatever approach is used, it helps to have a personal letter kept with your other important documents. Your note can detail what you want to have happen and ask the family to abide by your wishes.

Hartnett suggests, "Spell out, 'This is what I want to have happen, it's something I really want to do.' That way the family knows that you actually thought about it, it's not just something listed in the trust or the will. It's something that you really mean and it's a personal thing. People tend not to want to go against someone's true last wishes."

What if someone dies without a will or trust?

If you don't have a will, the state has one for you that dictates which relatives get your assets, whether you want those folks to get your stuff or not. Each state in the US has intestacy statutes that say how assets will be divided upon your death if you don't have a will.

While this varies from state to state, the line of succession usually goes to spouse and kids, parents, siblings, and depending on who's alive or dead, on to grandparents and/or nieces and nephews.

"Let's say that you are not married, have no kids, and your parents are dead, so everything would go equally to your siblings. Well, maybe you don't like your siblings or you have a significant other that you really want your assets to go to. Without a will or other arrangements, your assets would all go to your siblings," said Steve Hartnett with the American Academy of Estate Planning Attorneys.

A will overrides intestacy, specifying how you want to distribute assets that are titled in your name at death. Having a will does not avoid probate court, however.

"The process that is used to change the title from the name of someone who died to the new people is called probate. That's the administration of the assets at death, and that can be a time-consuming and potentially expensive process depending on the state," explained Hartnett.

Revocable living trusts are used by estate planning attorneys to avoid having assets go through probate, such as a house, brokerage account, or business. A trust can also provide for you in the event of incapacitation, such as a coma, that makes you unable to manage your affairs.

If you become incapacitated, your successor trustee can step in and manage those assets for you in a very simple process that requires a physician's certification. At your death, the trust divides up the assets the way you want it done.

Other ways to avoid probate include different forms of ownership, depending on the state. With joint tenancy in the ownership of the home, the property would pass to the surviving joint tenant, who is usually the spouse, but there can be income tax, estate tax, and asset protection issues.

Beneficiary designations in 401Ks and IRAs go automatically to the person named as the beneficiary. In many states, a bank account can also be set up as a Transfer on Death Account (TOD) that goes directly to the person named as the beneficiary.

"It's important to work with an attorney who's experienced in estate planning issues," said Hartnett. "It's a very complicated area, not something that you can just dabble in and be effective. Thousands of laws change each year that impact on estate planning and it takes a lot to stay up on it."

What if there's a funeral and we have children? Should we bring them?

The psychologists and counselors I've met through the Association for Death Education and Counseling cite studies and anecdotal evidence that children who attend funerals grow up to be well-adjusted adults. It's often the kids kept away from funerals by well-meaning parents seeking to protect them who may run into problems with grief issues later.

According to grief counselor Joan Guntzelman, bringing children to funerals is perfectly fine, with some preparation on the part of the parents.

Using teachable moments, such as the death of a pet, seeing an animal dead on the side of the road, or observing a plant that has died, can be a good way of showing a child that death is a part of life and it happens to all living things. Guntzelman suggests parents can say to the child, "It can be hard, because this plant, animal, or person will be missed."

"It's always a good idea for parents to explain death to kids in ways they can comprehend," said Guntzelman. "Be careful about explaining death in terms of God taking a person away, because developmentally, that's a concept many little ones have not mastered yet, or of saying things like, 'Grandpa's sleeping now.' When you try to get them to go to sleep, they may react with anxiety or even terror."

It's okay for an adult to express sadness to a child over the loss of a loved one. Kids learn mostly by identification and imitation, so when they see an adult grieving, they absorb how it's done. It's important for grown-ups, as well.

"Nobody expects you to do this with a big smile on your face," said Guntzelman. "The way we humans incorporate loss into our lives is the process of grieving. It's fine to cry. It's part of the way we express our relationship with this person."

"Never force a child to kiss a corpse. If they want to kiss Grandpa, or touch his hand, or put one of their toys in the casket, that's fine," said Guntzelman. "Kids' memories are more images and experiences rather than what people say to them."

"As long as they understand first where they're going and the parents talk to them according to their age level about what's happened here, children are fine going to funerals," Guntzelman explained. "Kids can take almost anything as long as they have closeness, warmth and support while they're doing it."

What if a child dies?

The death of a child is wrenching, whether from accident, illness, or other causes. It's out of order in the cycle of life and death. The young are not supposed to die before the old.

Counselor Guntzelman, who has years of experience working with grieving families, notes, "With any child's death, there's a huge sense of sadness and often guilt and responsibility on the part of the parents, a feeling of 'I failed' or 'I didn't do it right.' It may take a long time for a parent to come to self-forgiveness for the death or illness of a child."

Marriages can have problems after the death of a child because men and women often grieve differently.

When a child dies, while the same paperwork and disposition choices need to be made as for an adult, you don't want the funeral to look or sound like one for an old person. The accoutrements of childhood, such as favorite toys, stories, poetry, music, or flowers, can be displayed and utilized at the event.

Plan the service with input from the children who will be there. You'll want to let the funeral director and your clergy person know about any special plans you have and find out if they are willing to be involved. Think about what kind of service would be most personal and meaningful to you and your family.

The family might consider holding a funeral service geared to children, separate from an "adult" funeral. Contact the parents of the children to be invited and let them know what you are planning. A counselor or other caring adult can talk with the kids and help them share their stories about the deceased, process their grief and generate understanding.

One helpful strategy is to provide crayons and paper for the children to make artistic expressions of their feelings after a funeral, whether the event was for an adult or a child.

What if someone dies and "it's complicated"?

Relationships with family and the deceased can be complicated by a sudden, unexpected death, ambivalent feelings toward the deceased, and unresolved situations. Guntzelman offered her insights into complicated grief situations.

"Death is always a time of disbelief anyway, but when it comes as an unexpected shock, the family may have lots of unfinished business," said Guntzelman. "The hardest grieving is when people didn't work out their problems, didn't apologize, or whatever it might be that they needed to do."

Some of the most difficult grief to deal with involves ambivalent relationships, such as when you love someone 45 percent of the time and can't stand them 55 percent of the time. This "can't live with them, can't live without them" situation requires the bereaved to pay special attention to the negative side and address it internally to avoid future problems with unfinished business.

Guntzelman encourages creating a dialogue with the deceased person. Start by imagining the person is sitting in a chair next to you and talking with him or her, with you supplying both sides of the conversation.

She explained, "Even though the person is dead, you can still talk to them. Most of us believe that the spirit lives on in some way, and I know of many people who have been able to resolve their grief through these kinds of conversations."

When a person gradually declines toward their death because of age, illness, or disablement, anticipatory grieving sets in before the person dies. It can actually be a huge help, even though we don't realize it.

"Anticipatory grieving is a part of the natural human response, figuring out how we're going to keep on going without this person. It can also be a boon to the person who's dying, because then we can talk about it more openly," said Guntzelman. "When it's expected, there's time to ask for forgiveness. The biggest pain for many people who grieve is all the regrets, the 'if only I had' thoughts."

"If you have difficult relationships, it's important to be sure it's a 'clean' relationship, always clearing up unfinished business," she adds. "I can't tell you how many times people would say to me, 'I never told him I loved him. I should have told him more that I loved him.' After all my work with dying folks, whenever I talk to anybody in my family, before I hang up the phone, I always say, I love you."

11

As Time Goes By

Remembering the deceased

"The secret of a good memory is attention,
and attention to a subject depends upon our interest in it.
We rarely forget that which has made a deep impression on our minds."
— Tryon Edwards, 1809–1894

Every January 10, March 16, May 4, and November 2, I light a candle in memory of Grandma Dot, Grandma Min, Grandpa Ben, and Grandpa Phil. I put a picture on my kitchen table, and light a twenty-four-hour candle next to it the evening before. For that day, I imagine that particular grandparent sitting in with my husband and me as we go about our business and talk about our day.

It's as if they get a glimpse into our current lives and I feel their presence for that day. We do the same for my husband's grandparents, cousin, and father, and for other people we have loved and lost.

Even though the death of a loved one is devastating, life does go on. The anniversary of that death provides opportunities to reflect and remember. Throughout the year, at holidays and special times, the act of remembrance keeps departed loved ones alive within our hearts.

Anniversary Candle Lighting

Lighting a candle on the anniversary of a loved one's death has power. It's a tradition in Jewish households, as well as in Catholic churches. Those without a faith tradition, or whose religion does not call for annual recognition, can benefit from this simple candle lighting tradition.

The days I light candles for my grandparents correspond to the days they died. This tradition is called a *yartzeit*, a word with German roots. The act of remembering these dates and lighting these candles reminds me of their positive traits, their shortcomings, the fact that they raised my parents who in turn raised me, the intertwining of their influence throughout the generations.

Remembrance candles can also be lit for the departed on their birthdays, anniversaries, holidays, any time you want to make a special effort to call forth their spirits. The burning flame, representing the eternal, enduring spirit, can provide a sense of comfort at the times we most miss our dearly departed.

Memorial Obituaries

Another annual memorial option: take out an obituary posting in the newspaper. Scattered among the announcements of funerals and memorial services, you find entries that recall loved ones who died on the same date. Some died only a year earlier, but others salute those who have been gone for many years. A memorial obit can also be placed on birthdays, anniversaries, or holidays.

These "In Memoriam" listings can be straightforward statements of love and longing, or mystical quotations of poetry and song that only those closest to the deceased can appreciate. As with a classified obituary for a funeral, the family pays for the placement of these remembrances.

Typical memorial announcements include the deceased's name, the date of birth and death, a statement along the lines of "gone but not forgotten," any special thoughts about the individual, and ending with an indication of who is missing this person, such as "Mom and Dad," "your family and friends," or a nickname only the deceased would know.

Cemetery Visits

Many religions incorporate visits to cemeteries to honor the dead throughout the cycle of the year. Hispanic Catholics will decorate graves at holidays and picnic next to loved ones' final resting places. Jews leave a stone at the grave with each visit, an enduring marker indicating the living care about the dead. Some Romanian Orthodox will hold dinners at the grave of loved ones. Bringing flowers on holidays or anniversaries is a common tribute in many religious and cultural traditions.

Holiday Observances

The traditions that accompany family-centric holidays make the loss of a family member much more painful. In our family, we have a tradition of prominently placing large pictures in the dining room of those who have died, so they are, in a sense, present as the whole family enjoys the holiday meal. This is an option that acknowledges the person's passing while continuing to observe family annual events.

One Christmas season, a woman at a holiday party told of her fifty-six-year-old son who died of a heart attack on Christmas Day the year before. She and her daughter-in-law planned to go out of town for the holiday and do something completely different. This is a healthy response — to strike out in a new direction on a tradition-laden day when a loved one is no longer present. It recognizes the "new normal" all families face as they go through mourning, processing grief as time passes.

On birthdays, anniversaries, Mother's Day, Father's Day, and any day special to the family, acknowledging the deceased is not morbid or unnatural. It's okay to share memories. That loved one is already on everyone's mind.

Roadside Memorials

Descanso is a Spanish word meaning rest or resting place. It is also a roadside marker that indicates where a person died in an automobile accident. *Descansos* are plentiful throughout the Southwest and are showing up along highways throughout the United States. Family of the deceased may decorate these markers throughout the year, changing the items to reflect the season. The regulations regarding the legality of these roadside memorials vary by state. Some highway departments see them as distractions, others as expressions of cultural heritage.

Household Shrines

Small family shrines within the home paying homage to ancestors are common within Eastern religions such as Hinduism, Buddhism, and Shinto. Roman Catholic, Islamic, and Wiccan or Pagan families also have traditions of religious shrines in the home. However, an altar or niche dedicated to the memory of loved ones does not need to have a religious overtone to bring a sacred space into everyday life.

Elements of a personal family shrine can include cremated remains, photos of the deceased, and objects associated with those who have died. The placement of the shrine can be on a shelf, a tabletop, a mantle, a niche, or any place that can serve as a visual focus. Some families go as far as dedicating a room as a home chapel or meditation space to honor their ancestors and loved ones.

Possible activities with a family shrine include burning candles and incense, placing flowers or food, and taking time to meditate about the deceased. All of these can help individuals to center themselves and process their grief any time of the year.

About Day of the Dead Observances

The Day of the Dead celebrations held on November 1 and 2 acknowledge the culmination of the life cycle, and that death will come to us all. While it directly follows Halloween, the holiday is not designed to scare or bring sadness.

The Day of the Dead allows the living to honor those who have died — family, friends, ancestors, and pets. While its origins are from ancient Mesoamerican cultures, which range from Mexico to Honduras and El Salvador, anyone can adopt this annual observance and tailor this colorful celebration to remember their own deceased loved ones.

History

Starting with the Halloween connection, going back about 3,000 years, the ancient Celtic people believed that on October 31 the boundary between the living and the dead dissolve, allowing spirits of the deceased to cross over into the living world.

To combat the Druid festival *Samhain* (pronounced Sow-wen) held this time of the year, the Catholic Church moved All Saints' Day — a.k.a. All Hallows' Day — from mid-May to November 1. Halloween comes from abbreviating All Hallows' Even, the evening before the day.

Meanwhile, over in the Western Hemisphere, indigenous peoples such as the Aztec, Maya, Olmec, Toltec, and other tribes in Mexico held rituals celebrating the deaths of ancestors during the month of August. It corresponded with a festival dedicated to a goddess called *Mictecacihuatl*, The Lady of the Dead. When Catholic Spanish Conquistadors came to the New World more than 500 years ago, they tried to eradicate these native rituals that seemed to mock death and symbolized death and rebirth.

The ancient rituals refused to die in the face of forced conversion. So to make the ritual more Christian, the Spaniards moved it to correspond with All Saints' Day and All Souls' Day, November 1 and 2. In Mexico, *Dia De Los Muertos*, as it is known in Spanish, often honors deceased children and infants on the first day, and deceased adults on the second day.

The early Mesoamerican attitude was that life is a dream, and death is the awakening to real life. The dead are considered to have semidivine status, given permission to return once a year. They are to be welcomed, not feared.

How Day of the Dead is Celebrated

Today, Day of the Dead celebrations are held in Mexico, parts of Central and Latin America, in the Southwest US, and some European countries. In Mexico, the celebrations are elaborate, even more so than Christmas observances. Parades and profuse decorations in homes and cemeteries make this time of the year a tourist spectacle.

Families visit cemeteries to clean the graves of loved ones, decorate them with flowers and candles, and commune with the spirits of the departed. Often, they picnic in the cemetery, bringing the deceased's favorite food and drink.

When the Church granted magical curative powers to relics, it was extended to the use of *milagros*, Spanish for miracles, metal charms in the shape of body parts that need healing. This gave rise to specially shaped Day of the Dead foods, such as sugar skulls and *pan de muerto*, sweet egg bread baked in the shape of skulls or bones. These can be offerings to the dead or eaten by the living.

Colorful parades are held with people dressed as skeletons, a reminder that in death, we actually continue life. Skull masks and artwork of skeletons doing everyday activities, such as dancing, bicycle riding, and eating and drinking, remind us that the everlasting soul continues on, separate from the body.

The celebration continues in the home, welcoming the dead with respect and devotion. Some families will make an elaborate dinner, set out the food and not eat it until the next day, to let the spirits eat first. They may also make the bed with fresh sheets to allow the spirits to rest after their long journey to earth. And they construct *ofrendas*, individualized altars with offerings to maintain relations with the dead.

Making an *Ofrenda* or Altar

You don't have to be Mexican or Catholic to honor your loved ones with a Day of the Dead altar in your home and welcome their spirits for a visit. Start by setting up a table with photos of the deceased, and their ashes if you have them. Don't forget to include departed pets!

Decorate around the photos with flowers and candles. Set out foods and beverages that they used to enjoy. Play the music they loved. Put art objects they collected or artwork they created on or near the altar. Write messages to them and place the notes next to their photos. Include items from pets' lives, such as toys, leashes, treats, and tags.

Traditional *ofrendas* have items that represent the four elements of earth, air, fire, and water. A glass of water is included to give the spirits a drink after their long journey. Tissue paper sheets with elaborate cutout designs, called *papel picado*, represent air, as they move with the gentlest breeze. Flowers and a bowl of salt often represent the earth, and candles provide fire.

Marigolds are the flower of choice for Day of the Dead decorations. Their pungent scent is said to guide souls to earth, and marigolds are often still blooming in late October. Flowers can be arranged in an arch, along with sheets of *papel picado*, representing the connection from earth to heaven.

Create the altar prior to Halloween, and keep it up for as long as it feels right. Photograph the altar for posterity. Each year presents a new opportunity to remember and honor those who meant so much to us while they lived. Inevitably, there will be new faces to add as the years go by.

12

Just the Facts

Planning forms and online resources

*"Facts are stubborn things; and whatever may be our wishes,
our inclinations, or the dictates of our passion,
they cannot alter the state of facts and evidence."*
— *John Adams, second US President (1735–1826)*

This is not your grandfather's funeral planning form. You can download a complimentary Word document file of this information to complete and save for your family by visiting the website www.AGoodGoodbye.com and entering your name and email in the box for the free planner.

It's a good idea to fill out at least The Big Stuff information for yourself, your spouse or significant other, your living parents, your kids, and for any siblings, if you might be put in a position to plan a funeral on their behalf.

The Big Stuff Needed for a Death Certificate in the US (Includes the Five Things You Need to Know Now Before Someone Dies)

Full Name (official first, middle and last on birth certificate):

Nick Name (what your friends usually call you):

Maiden Name (if female):

Date of Birth (month/day/year):

Place of Birth (city and state or foreign country):

Social Security Number:

Residence Address (street, city, state, zip):

Sex (male or female):

Father's Full Name:

Mother's Full Maiden Name (better know this!):

Marital Status (check one):

__ single __ married __ divorced __ widow/widower

Surviving Spouse's Name (if wife, include maiden name):

Served in US Armed Forces (yes or no):

Preferred Method of Disposition:

Race:

Highest level of education:

Usual occupation (kind of work during career):

Veteran Information (Thanks for your service! We salute you.)

Service/Branch:

Date and Place of Enlistment:

Date of Discharge:

Rank and Service Number:

Veterans' Administration Claim Number:

War/Conflicts/Tours of Duty:

Commendations Received:

Marital History
Current Marriage (to full name and date):

Previous Marriages (Names, dates of wedding and divorce finalization, current address and phone number of ex, notes):

Religious information
If atheist or agnostic, you can skip this section or write down what friend(s) you'd like to conduct a memorial service and where you'd like it held.

Religion:

House of Worship:

Address and Telephone:

Clergy to Contact:

Codes, Combinations, and Online Passwords

Mark down user name and passwords for key online activities. Remaining live online after your demise can be problematic for your survivors. Note other codes or combinations needed to access important information.

Computer log-on or administrative access:

Internet Service Provider:

Email Provider:

Facebook Account:

Twitter Account:

Cell Phone Account:

Burglar Alarm Code/Password:

Online Banking/Investment Accounts:

Online Merchant Accounts (i.e., Amazon, catalogues, stores):

Website(s) Administration:

Safe Combination:

Family to Notify

When time is of the essence, can you easily assemble the names, addresses, emails and phone numbers for all your family and friends? *The Family Plot File* is an electronic data resource that will make contacting your family and friends so much easier and help smooth the way to a successful event.

Download your copy through the planner section of the Stuff To Die For link at www.AGoodGoodbye.com

Spouse:

Parent:

Parent:

Child:

Child:

Child:

Child:

Grandchild:

Grandchild:

Grandchild:

Grandchild:

Grandchild:

Grandchild:

Sibling:

Sibling:

Sibling:

Sibling:

Sibling:

Friends and Others to Notify

Name, Telephone, Email:

Name, Telephone, Email:

Name, Telephone, Email:

Name, Telephone, Email:

Name, Telephone, Email:

Name, Telephone, Email:

Name, Telephone, Email:

Name, Telephone, Email:

Name, Telephone, Email:

Name, Telephone, Email:

Name, Telephone, Email:

Name, Telephone, Email:

Executor (Name, address, telephone, email)

Insurance Agent/Company (Name, address, telephone, email)

Attorney (Name, address, telephone, email)

Financial Advisor/CPA (Name, address, telephone, email)

Other Professional Advisors (Name, address, telephone, email)

Obit News Bits

In addition to helping draft an informative obituary, these details can be used to notify other people who will want to know about the death.

Education (Include name of school, city and state, degree earned, dates attended.)

High School:

Community College or Trade School:

University:

Graduate Degree(s):

Membership in Alumni Association(s):

Career Highlights (Note companies worked for and dates, achievements, awards, etc.)

Hobbies and Interests (Note any pursuits or passions that play a large role in life.)

Organizations to Contact

This is helpful to alert people who may be involved in your professional, community, or volunteer life. This can include unions, fraternal organizations, professional interest groups, volunteer services, and other community contacts.

List the name of the organization, address, telephone, and if possible, a specific contact person. If no longer a member, you may want to note the dates of membership. Note if you'd like to name one of these organizations as a memorial donation beneficiary.

Organization:

Organization:

Organization:

Organization:

Organization:

Newspapers or Publications for Obituary

List the local newspapers or trade publications that would be appropriate for either a paid obituary announcement or a news obit. Having the publication name, telephone, and website address handy is one less thing to stress about.

Publication:

Publication:

Publication:

Publication:

Publication:

Document Locator

Let your family know where the important documents are kept. Here's a quick rundown of what documents and other information your family will need to put their hands on if there's a medical emergency or death. Note "yes or no" regarding each piece: where it's located, an account number or other reference as needed, and any other notes.

Will:

Living Will:

Living Trust:

Medical Power of Attorney:

Durable Power of Attorney:

Cemetery Plot Deed:

Body/Organ Donor Information:

Safe Deposit Box:

Safe Deposit Box Key:

P.O. Box:

P.O. Box Key:

Automobile Title(s):

Birth Certificate:

Passport:

Divorce Papers:

Life Insurance:

Health Insurance:

Long-Term Care or Disability Insurance:

Auto/Home Insurance:

Savings Accounts:

Checking Accounts/Checkbooks:

Credit Cards (account numbers, toll-free phone):

Annuities:

Mortgage Papers/Deeds:

Income Tax Records:

Retirement Plans:

Government Benefit Statements:

Your Final Wishes

Sketch out what you envision for your Good Goodbye. Fill in responses as appropriate.

Pre-need arrangements made:

(if yes, name funeral provider and contact info):

Pre-need funding done (if yes, name company and contact info):

Disposition of Remains (Burial, cremation, body donation, other):

Prefer a funeral (body present) or a memorial service (cremains or not present):

Prefer a wake, viewing, picnic, wild party, other gathering:

If donating to science or medical school, list arrangements:

Cremated remains (Bury, scatter, keep in urn, columbarium, share with family, other):

Cemetery plot or mausoleum crypt purchased (list section, block, plot):

Casket preference (material and price range):

Open or closed casket:

Embalming preference (yes or no):

Clothing, jewelry, other burial item preferences (such as eyeglasses):

Marker preference (headstone or plaque):

Epitaph/words of wisdom:

Location of funeral/memorial service:

Favorite flowers:

Memorial gifts in lieu of flowers:

Officiating clergy or friends:

Speakers – eulogy and readers:

Readings:

Music selections, musical instruments:

Casket bearers:

Honorary pallbearers:

Other special instructions:

Party Planning Checklist

For almost any type of entertaining, consider having the following items on hand in sufficient quantities for the expected number of guests. Depending on the formality of the event, plates, cups, glasses, utensils, and tablecloths can range from fine china, crystal, silver, and linen to paper and plastic goods. Depending on the menu, you may not need all items.

Party Item Checklist

- Plates – formal dining includes salad and bread plates
- Dessert plates
- Cups and saucers or mugs for coffee or tea
- Bowls – if serving soup, chili, stews, or other liquid-based dishes
- Wine glasses – specific to the type of wine being served, such as red, white, or champagne
- Beer glasses – mugs, pub, or Pilsner glasses
- Water glasses
- Eating utensils – forks for salad, the main course, and dessert, soup spoons, tea spoons, knives, specialty utensils as dictated by the menu
- Serving utensils – large spoons, forks, salad tongs, gravy spoon, cutting and serving pieces for desserts
- Serving china – platters, bowls, gravy boat, items determined by the menu
- Tablecloth(s) or placemats
- Napkins – sized for beverages, as well as luncheon or dinner settings
- Coffee urn and/or hot water for tea – consider offering both regular and decaffeinated options

- Coffee service items – sugar and/or low-calorie sweeteners, milk and/or nondairy creamer, honey, lemon for tea, stirrers
- Condiments – salt and pepper, others as appropriate for the menu, such as mustard, mayonnaise, ketchup, salad dressings, soy sauce, etc.
- Chairs – enough seating capacity for the number of guests expected
- Tables – unless it's a cocktail party where people are eating standing up or sitting around the living room, make sure the dining table is big enough for the expected guests, or that additional tables are available.
- Buffet warming trays or chafing dishes
- Extension cords or power strips for electric appliances
- Table decorations – candles, flowers, thematic decorative items
- Matches or lighters for lighting candles
- Place card markers for assigned seating

Online Resources for Information and Services

American Academy of Estate Planning Attorneys:
www.AAEPA.com

American Association of Tissue Banks: www.AATB.org

Association for Death Education and Counseling:
www.ADEC.org

Association for Pet Loss and Bereavement: www.APLB.org

Crossings – Home death care information: www.Crossings.net

Cremation Association of North America:
www.CremationAssociation.org

Engage With Grace – The five questions to start a conversation
on advance medical directives:
www.EngageWithGrace.org

Everest Funeral Planning and Concierge Services:
www.EverestFuneral.com

The Family Plot Blog – Funeral planning for those who don't
plan to die: TheFamilyPlot.wordpress.com

The Federal Trade Commission – Consumer information on
funerals:
www.FTC.gov/bcp/edu/microsites/funerals/coninfo.htm

Five Wishes – A booklet for expressing advance medical
directives: www.AgingWithDignity.org

Funeral Consumers Alliance – Ensuring consumers can choose a
meaningful, dignified, and affordable funeral:
www.Funerals.org

Funeralwise.com – Everything you need to know about
funerals: www.Funeralwise.com

Geib Funeral Home Blog: www.AskTheDirector.net

Goliath Casket Company – Standing in the Gap for the Big and Tall: www.OversizeCasket.com

Good Funeral Guide – A UK-based blog and independent consumer guide to funerals: www.GoodFuneralGuide.co.uk

Green Burial Council – Environmentally sustainable death care: www.GreenBurial.org

International Association of Pet Cemeteries and Crematories: www.IAOPC.com

International Cemetery, Cremation and Funeral Association: www.ICCFA.com

National Funeral Directors Association: www.NFDA.org

Selected Independent Funeral Homes: www.SelectedFuneralHomes.org

Your Funeral Guy – Funeral news with the consumer in mind: YourFuneralGuy.wordpress.com

Special Offer: *The Family Plot File*

At Last! You Can Organize Personal Contacts for Major Life Events Without Losing Your Mind

When time is of the essence, can you easily assemble the names, addresses, emails, and phone numbers for all your family and friends?

If your current personal list consists of Mom's dog-eared personal phone book or phone numbers programmed into your cell phone, you may have problems keeping track of everyone you have contacted or need to contact, whether it's good news or bad.

Organization is the key to successfully implement life cycle events, such as weddings and funerals, without losing your mind.

By utilizing *The Family Plot File*, this electronic data resource will make contacting your family and friends so much easier!

Here's how *The Family Plot File* can help smooth the way to a successful event:

- Keeps all your current contact information in one place
- Updates easily as contact information changes
- Create different lists — phone, email, or mailing
- Make mailing labels for invitations or holiday cards
- Customize contact lists by different groups — family, friends, work, interests, etc.
- Track contact history — cards, calls, thank you notes, etc.

The Family Plot File provides electronic template forms in Word and Excel formats, including a Master List, Telephone and Email Contacts, Mailing Labels, and easy-to-follow instructions.

The Family Plot File is available for $29.97. Use this order form or order online today at www.AGoodGoodbye.com.

Yes! I want to organize my personal contacts! Please send me *The Family Plot File*.

Name: _____

Address: _____

City, State, Zip: _____

Email: _____

Phone: _____

[ ] **Enclosed is my check to Gail Rubin for $29.97**

[ ] **Please charge my credit card: Visa MasterCard American Express Discover**
Card # _____ **Expiration Date** _____ **Security Code** ____
Signature:

_____

Mail order form to:

Light Tree Press
P.O. Box 36987
Albuquerque, NM 87176-6987

About the Author

Gail Rubin is an event planner specializing in funerals and memorial services. She's also the author of The Family Plot Blog: Funeral Planning for Those Who Don't Plan to Die.

She started the blog after writing "Matchings, Hatchings, and Dispatchings," a local newspaper feature on life cycle events. She found that the articles on death elicited reader responses that indicated a need for more information. The Family Plot Blog (TheFamilyPlot.wordpress.com) provides the information, inspiration, and tools to preplan creative and meaningful end-of-life events.

A breast cancer survivor, she is a member of the Association for Death Education and Counseling, the cemetery committee for Congregation Albert in Albuquerque, New Mexico, and a member of the *Chevra Kaddisha*, a volunteer organization that ritually prepares the bodies of Jews for burial.

Gail Rubin speaks to groups about funeral planning and helps get the conversation started. For more information and resources, visit www.AGoodGoodbye.com.

CPSIA information can be obtained
at www.ICGtesting.com
Printed in the USA
LVOW13s2340190217
524782LV00004B/14/P